The Complete Guide to
Learning a Language

Thank you for buying one of our books. We hope you'll enjoy the book, and that it will help you achieve your goal of learning another language.

We always try to ensure our books are up to date, but contact details seem to change so quickly that it can be very hard to keep up with them. If you do have problems contacting any of the organisations listed at the back of the book please get in touch, and either we or the author will do what we can to help. And if you do find contact details that differ from those in the book, please let us know so that we can put it right when we reprint.

Please do also give us your feedback so we can go on making books that you want to read. If there's anything you particularly liked about this book – or you have suggestions about how it could be improved in the future – email us on info@howtobooks.co.uk

The Publishers
www.howtobooks.co.uk

If you want to know how ...

Practical Research Methods
A user-friendly, six stage guide to mastering research

Critical Thinking for Students
Learn the skills of critical assessment and effective argument

Writing an Assignment
Proven techniques from a chief examiner that really get results

Writing Your Dissertation
The bestselling guide to planning, preparing and presenting first-class work

howtobooks

Please send for a free copy of the latest catalogue to:

How To Books
3 Newtec Place, Magdalen Road
Oxford OX4 1RE, United Kingdom
email: info@howtobooks.co.uk
www.howtobooks.co.uk

The Complete Guide to

Learning a Language

How to learn a language with the least amount of difficulty
and the most amount of fun

Gill James

how tobooks

Published by How To Books Ltd,
3 Newtec Place, Magdalen Road,
Oxford OX4 1RE, United Kingdom.
Tel: (01865) 793806. Fax: (01865) 248780.
email: info@howtobooks.co.uk
http://www.howtobooks.co.uk

British Library Cataloguing in Publication Data.
A catalogue record for this book is available from
the British Library.

Produced for How To Books by Deer Park Productions
Typeset by Kestrel Data, Exeter, Devon
Cover design by Baseline Arts Ltd, Oxford
Printed and bound by Cromwell Press Ltd, Trowbridge, Wiltshire

NOTE: The material contained in this book is set out in good
faith for general guidance and no liability can be accepted
for loss or expense incurred as a result of relying in particular
circumstances on statements made in the book. Laws and
regulations are complex and liable to change, and readers should
check the current position with the relevant authorities before
making personal arrangements.

Contents

language and the cultural insights that that brings? It might be time to reassess your goals and consider a new learning style.

You have attained the goals identified in Chapter 1 and have decided to either go further or maintain your language at the level you have reached. Now you need some strategies for continuing to learn your language without even noticing.

Preface

It was the bubble gum which started it for me. Little packs were sold at the tuck shop near to my primary school. A rectangular piece of card held the gum flat in its waxed paper pack. There was a national flag printed on one side of the card, on the other a few useful phrases from the language of the country involved. How our journeys to school were enhanced as we practised on each other the phrases we had acquired from last night's chewing! Woe betide he or she who had not chewed enough to know that '*Tengo ocho años*' was a statement about your age and not an invitation to a sexy Latin American dance.

Then came the delights of the *Children's Encyclopaedia*. Many a Sunday morning, whilst my parents had a lie-in, was spent skipping from section to section finding the stories in French, which were well illustrated, and translated into English below. And delight of delights, sandwiched between the French and the English, a phonetic spelling of how the French sounded. Reading it aloud, taking on the roles of the various characters was such fun!

Not that it has always been joyful. That moment of panic, at the end of the first year in secondary school, when I told myself that I knew very little French, even though I had performed well in every lesson and in every piece of home-work. Being plunged into the deep end of A-level German after just two years of two lessons a week, and struggling for three hours with the first piece of homework. Being tongue-tied on my first visit to France, even though I had been learning French for a long time.

But there have been times of great joy. Like seeing my own pupils, just at the end of their second year of French, cope with following directions, ordering food and shopping in French. No, they did more than cope. They performed. When I was a student myself and worked in a small group, we were often joined by the German assistant. Two teachers, therefore, to three pupils. We discussed everything under the sun, put the world right and read not just the set books, but everything of significance written by the authors con-cerned. And then some. We stopped noticing it was a foreign language. Or my own son, on our return to England after living for two years in Holland, complaining that the other kids didn't understand the extra bits of language he could use. He meant the Dutch he had acquired by playing with other children from our street.

Gradually, gradually, over the years, I have noticed what actually makes it happen, what makes it all come together. Recently, I have been able to put that into practice with my private pupils, and have been astonished and delighted by the results. If only I had known all this sooner! When I first started on my own language learning for instance or when I started teaching others. We would have attained our goals more rapidly. I hope this book will offer you a short cut.

But the fun doesn't have to stop there. My level of understanding and appreciation in all of my languages is way beyond what I had hoped for in the bubble gum days or even had aspired to in obtaining a degree. I now have many meaningful friendships with speakers of other languages. The process does not end. Instead, you go in deeper and deeper until, aided by your willingness to understand, you touch the very soul of the other.

Gill James

1

What's in It for Me?

In this chapter you are invited to work out:

◆ why you are learning a language

◆ what you want to be able to do by the end of your course

◆ how much time you can give to your study

◆ whether your expectations are realistic

◆ how to know when you are succeeding.

REASONS FOR LEARNING

The usual reasons for learning a foreign language are many and varied.

1. **You may, for example, be asked to learn a new language for your company.** It may make sense to learn German if you are working for BMW, but may seem less appropriate for Ford. In theory, though, we are expected to sell to customers in their home land and through their language. In practice, we tend to employ native speakers of that language to do our selling. But here's a thought. Who sells best, a linguist with no selling skills, or a sales manager who has acquired some foreign language?

2. **You may have work contacts abroad where it would be useful to speak their language.** My husband decided to learn Dutch because a lot of Dutch colleagues came to his meetings in England. There was very little problem with communication. Most Dutch people speak fluent English anyway. But they did have the irritating habit of having a meeting after the meeting in their own language. It was very threatening to those people who did not understand them. So, my husband took himself off to evening class, and at the next meeting was able to understand a fair amount of what they were saying. None of it was threatening in fact, but it would have been useful if they had shared their afterthoughts with everyone. He then spoke to them in quite sophisticated Dutch, using a phrase he had learnt especially for the occasion. They didn't know that of course, and were duly impressed. After that, they expressed their last minute considerations in English to everyone or in Dutch to my husband. The meetings became more useful generally.

3. **You may need an extra qualification.** A GCSE or similar in a language may be good. Perhaps you didn't manage that at school. A good pass in a language is still the most respected after English, maths, science and any other subject you may wish to study in higher education. Students entering primary education training in Great Britain now have to have a good pass in their first foreign language – they're going to have to teach it soon!

4. **You may be going to live abroad, or perhaps you holiday frequently or have a holiday home in a certain country.** It is more fun if you can communicate with the people who live there. But you will probably need to learn an entirely

different sort of language from the man who is trying to sell an American car produced in England to the Italians. That is why so often those of us who have done well in school find ourselves tongue-tied when we get out there; we learnt the wrong sort of French. And how far do you want to go? Do you just want to be able to cope with the shopping and understand the bills? Or do you want to be able to chat over the fence or over a nice bottle of the local wine, and put the world right?

5. **You may just enjoy languages.** You perhaps got on well with French at school. You liked getting your mouth around the words. The actor in you relished taking on a role. You were fascinated by the way language is structured. Now you want to take it further or you want to try out another language. Well, go for it!

Many people go to language classes to meet other people. I learnt Breton for that reason. I was doing the French part of my year abroad as a student. Unfortunately, they put all the foreign students together in a hall of residence. We communicated in French, but it wasn't French French. In order to meet French people, I joined a choir, played basketball and learnt Breton. And in learning Breton, I understood a lot more about the culture of Brittany and made many Breton-speaking friends.

You may join an adult education class to help pass lonely evenings and keep you in contact with other people if you lead an otherwise solitary life. That would also be true if you studied Chinese brush painting. But if you learn a foreign language there is also the exciting possibility of getting to know someone from another culture as well.

Often there is more than one reason or our reasons change as we go along. But if we are clear why we are learning, we can be clear about what we want from our course, and choose the right one.

ANALYSE YOUR REASONS FOR LEARNING

Study the list below. Award each reason marks out of five. 0 = not relevant, 5 = a very strong reason. In brackets I have put the marks I gave for learning Dutch as a guide.

◆ my firm wants me to learn it – I'm not sure why (0)

◆ I have work contacts with people who use this language (2)

◆ I would like an extra qualification (1)

◆ I am going to live abroad (5)

◆ I go abroad a lot on holiday (3)

◆ I enjoy languages (3)

◆ I want to be sociable (4)

Now take the three reasons with the highest score and make them into a 'must' statement. If you have more than one with any of the three highest scores, include all of them. Hence my statement comes out as the following:

> **'We are going to live in Holland for two years. I want to make a lot of friends there, including Dutch ones. I always enjoy learning languages. I must learn enough Dutch in order to be able to do this.'**

If you have any statements left, make a 'might' statement from the next lowest:

> **'I might also work there and the contacts might be Dutch speaking.'**

Finally if you have anything left, do a 'could even' statement:

> **'I could even get another qualification in it if one exists that fits in with what I am doing.'**

WORKING OUT WHAT YOU WANT TO KNOW AND WILL BE ABLE TO DO

Now take your 'must' statement. Try to reduce it to note form. My 'must' came out as 'Enjoy living in Holland'. That statement is going to lead to a mind map which will help you to work out exactly what you are looking for in a language course. The mind map in Figure 1 shows my plans mind map for learning Dutch.

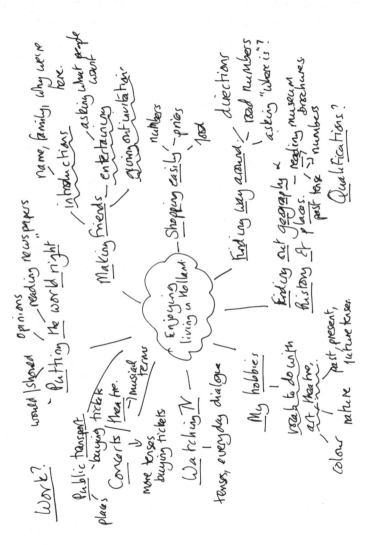

Fig. 1. Mind map 1.

To make a mind map, you put the 'must' statement in the middle of a 'cloud'. For the first branches going off, think what you actually might want to do, e.g. 'Finding my way around' . Think of as many things as you can and surround your cloud with them. Then break each one down into what that entails – in this case, understanding and giving directions, understanding and giving road numbers and asking 'where is?'. Carry on working until you have covered the page. You may like to use different colours or different fonts for different layers. There is a computer programme for writing mind maps – MindMan Personal for those who prefer to work with computers. I like feeling the pen on the paper at this planning stage.

In the top left-hand corner add a question to do with your 'might also' statement and in the bottom right one to do with your 'could even' statement.

You now have a checklist against which to assess the suitability of any course. If you choose an 'off the peg' course it is unlikely that you will get an exact match. The question at the top left-hand corner and the bottom right may help you to decide. If some of the mind map ideas are missing but one or both of those questions are answered, then the course you are looking at might be suitable.

FINDING THE TIME

We do have to be realistic. My mind map takes my Dutch up to quite a high level. As a linguist, I know full well that 'putting the world right' – being able to discuss politics, the World Cup and current affairs in a foreign language –

requires near native speaker skills. However, I had the advantage at the time of living in the country, which accelerates the learning process vastly and I already had most of the knowledge about language learning which I am now giving to you.

I almost made it. I hadn't yet worked out how to cope with the reluctance of the Dutch to let you struggle with their language, or how to respond when they answered my simple but perfectly formed question in a torrent. That is dealt with later in this book.

But even if you are not living in the country where your new language is spoken, you can create yourself more time. Consider the following:

◆ Getting up half an hour earlier.

◆ Going to bed half an hour later.

◆ Listening to a tape or CD whilst ironing, gardening, driving, exercising, walking the dog – or any other solitary activity you can think of.

◆ Watching TV for half an hour less a day.

◆ Spending 20 minutes (or another amount of time) of your lunch break.

◆ Converting some of your leisure time into something to do with your language e.g. watching French TV, reading an Italian magazine, listening to a German football commentary or looking at Dutch web sites.

◆ Socialising with a native speaker or other learner of your language in that language.

Now try this

Work out the total amount of time you can spend on your language.

1. Include the amount of time for formal lessons e.g. a two-hour class per week, three hours per week using the CD, or two half-hour sessions per week on a phone course.
2. Now write down what you can do for how long from the list above.
3. Add up the total amount of time.
4. Next, you need to work out how long it would take you to achieve everything on your mind map. Bear in mind that many professional actors learn their lines by reading the whole play 12 times through during three days. Think back to how long it took you to learn pieces of poetry or quotations at school. Each section on your mind map is going to take as long as learning a poem. Then you have learnt a pattern which is repeatable with other vocabulary – providing you learn that as well.

Following the suggestions in this book, with one hour per week formal instruction plus as much 'stolen' time as possible, most of my mind map is achievable in two years. The 'putting the world right' may take another two.

HOW DO I KNOW I AM SUCCEEDING?

Once a week look at your mind map. Tick off everything you know really well. Ring in pencil what you have met but are still not sure of. Put a pencil question mark by anything you have not covered in a given topic – e.g. I may feel that we have not completed enough number work to do with shopping.

Are you on target? If it is halfway through the time you have allowed, have you ticked half of the items off? Can you concentrate in your own learning time on those bits which you have ringed? If working with a teacher, can you ask for more work on that topic?

As the weeks go by, the rings and question marks should be turning into ticks.

The level of operational competence

This is my definition of a useful place to be. This is more fully explained in Appendix 1. Basically, you have enough skills in the language and enough knowledge of it to be able to make yourself understood and understand others in a variety of everyday situations. With a little more of a struggle, you can can chat on the 'putting the world right' level and you can write in a simplified form with anything you can write in your own language, but you will rely much more on dictionaries, grammar books and examples of writing in your chosen language.

Even if you are not studying a European language, you may find the European Languages Passport interesting. It has been developed by the Council of Europe. Some languages courses are registered for it, and you can have yourself assessed fairly formally through the scheme. It is quite a complex process and involves keeping a portfolio of your work.

The level descriptions can be very useful. There are six levels – A1, A2, B1, B2, C1, C2 in the areas of listening, reading, speaking (spoken interaction), speaking (spoken production) and writing. Level B1 is the equivalent of a good GCSE and of my level of operational competence, in my opinion achievable by everyone who follows this book, within two years of having one formal lesson a week, and is the level at which the language becomes realistically useful. This includes being able to understand speech on familiar matters, read texts containing everyday language, cope in everyday situations such as shopping, describe dreams and ambitions, narrate a simple story and write personal letters describing experiences and impressions. I would also say that level B1 is similar to the National Curriculm Level 6. The National Curriculum levels describe the performance of school children. See Appendix 1 for more details.

THE STORY SO FAR

◆ You have looked at why you want to learn a foreign language.

◆ You have worked out what you want to achieve.

◆ You have looked at how much time you can give.

◆ You know how to monitor your progress.

2

How Should I Learn?

In this chapter you:

◆ look at the different types of course which you can take

◆ look at the different settings where you can study your language

◆ look at your own learning style

◆ put together your own language course.

TYPES OF COURSE

There is a great variety of courses available. This section describes the different types of courses, their advantages and disadvantages, and which type of learner they suit.

Local authority classes

These take place in schools and adult education centres. They are one of the cheapest options. They are typically two hours per week, with a break in the middle, during term time. The pace is often quite gentle, unless you join an exam class. Many local authorities assign levels to different classes. These do to some extent mirror the levels for the European Passport. However, they do vary from area to area, so you need to check with the centre to find out what the various levels mean. In my area for example, Level 1 is for beginners. Level 7, where I went to a class in Spanish for many years, is post A-level. We were working towards degree-level language, but without the rigorous study of culture and literature.

Look out also for the Get-By series, which usually last about six weeks and give you just enough language to cope when you go on holiday.

Most of these courses are centred on a text book, so that if you have to miss a week you can catch up easily. Also, the teachers are usually very hard working and often produce many of their own handouts.

Advantages
Good value for money, usually good fun with end of term parties and trips out included. They are easy to find. They always use qualified tutors.

Disadvantages
Pace can sometimes be slow and may depend on other members of the group. Some schools and centres can be a bit grim, especially in the winter.

Learning style suited
For people who like learning in a group, and appreciate the discipline of having to attend every week, possibly completing some homework each time.

University continuing education departments

These are very similar to local authority classes, but are more demanding. They tend to be three hours per week, and a beginner's class would bring you up to that important level of operational competence (see Appendix 1), equivalent to a good GCSE and the first level at which you can really use the language usefully, within one year. They are a little more expensive than the local authority classes, but this just reflects the extra length of time. Again, they will often feature a course book and the tutor's own materials, but in both cases, these are harder.

Advantages

Highly qualified tutors are used. The pace is fast, and if you can keep up with the course, you will learn rapidly. As these are university based, you usually have access to good resources, including video labs and self study materials.

Disadvantages

The pace can be too fast sometimes, and there is a general assumption that the students understand languages and the language learning process.

Learning style suited

These courses suit people who already have competence in another language, perhaps at A-level or above. They would also be good for students who are learning just because they are interested in languages, and who want to make rapid progress.

Business language schools

There are many of these, and quality can vary. You need to

refer to your mind map to see whether one of these schools has a programme which will suit you. There are some well known names – Ceran, Berlitz and the Goethe Institute. All of these offer courses with qualifications which are recognised world-wide. They use very experienced teachers. The pace varies, according to which course you choose. Each course has very clear objectives and it is rare for a student not to attain the goals set.

Advantages
These courses are geared towards the business world. They have clear goals, which students usually meet. They tend to employ native speakers, who are well trained in the school's methods.

Disadvantages
They might suit business in general, not particularly your business. They can be very expensive.

Learning style suited
Anyone learning for business and who is expecting to make rapid progress. However, it is never just a matter of attending the lesson. You will be expected to so some work on your own. You may still be able to do this in your firm's time.

Tailor-made lessons
There are a few small language schools appearing now which offer tailor-made lessons. Your first contact with a teacher from such a school will be to establish why, what and how you want to learn. You will go through a similar process to what you are doing now and what you did in the previous chapter. Then your tutor negotiates with you what your

lessons will be like. There is also constant negotiation as you go along as to whether you are meeting your goals or whether you want to change them.

Many of these schools, like my own, Bridge House Languages, have been set up by individuals who have a wealth of experience in the world of foreign languages. They choose their tutors carefully, and give them ongoing training and support. Sometimes, they will actually recommend another type of course, either instead of or to supplement their own.

Advantages
You do get a course which suits you ideally. You can also take your lessons when and in which setting fits you best. You have a very personal relationship with your tutor.

Disadvantages
These courses can be expensive. You are having to pay the tutor not just for the time they are teaching you, but also for preparation time and in some cases travelling time. Even though cover is often offered if your tutor is ill or on holiday, many people prefer to stay with the same tutor, so many gaps can arise – especially if your commitments take you away at different times from your tutor.

Learning style suited
If you like to have a big say in what and how you learn, this type of course is for you. It will also suit you if you work unusual hours and have to travel frequently. You do need to be prepared to put in some work between lessons, if the course is to be effective.

Residential courses

These frequently take place in a country which speaks your target language. They are often quite formal courses and are certainly comprehensive and take you to a high standard quickly. You can try out your language more informally in the shops, bars and restaurants.

Advantages

These courses are by their very nature intensive. You learn a lot very quickly. You are taken out of your normal environment and have time to concentrate just on your language. If you regard them as a form of holiday, they are very good value for money.

Disadvantages

You may forget just as quickly as you learnt if you don't have the opportunity to carry on studying. All students are accommodated together, and even if you speak your target language amongst yourselves, it won't be proper Spanish or Greek.

Learning style suited

This will suit the type of person who likes to focus on one project at a time.

Home stay

These also take place in the country where your language is spoken. However, this time you stay with a family. In some cases, your lessons are given by a family member and even though from an 'off the peg' course, your tutor can gear them to your particular needs. In other cases, you actually go to an institution to meet with other students.

Advantages

You can learn a lot very quickly. You can make life-long friends at a very early stage of your learning. If regarded as a form of holiday, they are very good value for money.

Disadvantages

If you don't have the opportunity to carry on with your study, you can forget just as quickly. You will be sharing the home of another family and this is not always comfortable for everyone.

Learning style suited

This is ideal for those people who enjoy mixing with others, and who want to learn rapidly.

Going it alone

There are many courses available where you can work on your own. These are often based on books and CDs, such as the Linguaphone courses. There are now many computer-based programmes on CDs. Modern technology means that they are interactive and you get feed-back on how well you are doing. If you have the right sort of computer equipment – check on the software package that you have adequate hardware – sound files can be used easily, so that you even have practice at speaking and listening.

Advantages

You can work at your own pace, and where, when and as often as it suits you.

Disadvantages
You have no human feedback. You are working in isolation in an area where communication with other people is an important feature.

Learning style suited
If you have enough self-discipline, you can put yourself together your ideal language learning package. If you can work anywhere, for example if you are the sort of person who opens their lap-top on the train, then you will do very well with this sort of course. It will also suit you if you prefer to work on your own.

The Open University

The OU's courses combine many of the features of other universities' continuing education programmes and some of the 'go-it-alone' resources. You study with the aid of CDs, books, other printed materials and a video. You are linked to a tutor who supports you and assesses your work. Some courses include residential weeks – for example, the Summer School in Caen for the Level 2 French courses. The courses are fast-paced and hard-edged, and can lead to OU qualifications.

Advantages
You can to a large extent work when and as you choose, so this is useful if you work unusual hours. Highly qualified teachers are used. You do get some tutor support and deadlines, which help you to keep on target.

Disadvantages
You are working in isolation much of the time.

Learning style suited

This course will suit you if you like learning on your own, but need to have to report to someone so that you keep on task.

SETTINGS FOR LEARNING

Now you need to consider which of these settings suits you best. There may be more than one.

Working completely alone

The only feed-back that you get is from a tape or a computer. You pace yourself and you may have to force yourself to work. But you can work anywhere – at home, at the office, on the train, or whilst you are waiting for a plane.

One-to-one with a tutor

You have a tutor who works only with you and their attention is undivided. You can make fast progress, because only your learning needs are addressed. This can be very intimate or very claustrophobic, depending on your point of view.

In a small group

You are matched with people with very similar needs to your own. You can practise language patterns with other people in the group. You will have to go to some extent at the pace of the group rather than your own.

In a larger group

This course will probably be cheaper. It will be 'off the peg' and not entirely suited to your needs, but it will be an interesting group to work with.

On the phone

You work one-to-one with a tutor, usually very intensively for half an hour. This is not usually suitable for beginners. You can make good progress, and the lesson is absolutely geared to your needs. But you may never meet your tutor!

On-line/off-line

You complete tutorials via a computer, either in real time or in your own time. A human being assesses your work and gives you feedback. You may never meet this tutor. Again, this is not usually suitable for absolute beginners.

In your own home

The tutor comes to you, so you may have to shut the dog away and you might want to tidy up first. You will certainly need somewhere quiet to work. You may have to pay the tutor travelling expenses – this could be reflected in the price of your lesson. On the other hand, you won't incur any travelling costs or time.

In your tutor's home

Someone who teaches in their own home will usually have a designated space where you can work uninterrupted. Often they choose to work at home because they have many clients, and cannot afford to waste time travelling. And they probably have lots of clients because they are very good. They will also have extra resources for you readily to hand.

In your office

A great boon if it is the company who are paying because they want you to learn that language. You are at least then not using your own time for the lesson. Tutors who come to offices are usually very professional.

In an adult education centre

The centre will have taken some care in assessing the level at which you should study. These centres often have other facilities to support the student – such as a crèche, a coffee bar, and news about other events, such as theatre trips and end of term parties.

In university continuing education departments

These will often have the same facilities as adult education centres, but also provide students with access to IT rooms, libraries, and video and language labs.

CHOOSING THE RIGHT TYPE OF COURSE

You may have a clear view now of what type of courses are on offer, and which ones you like and in which settings you could work. If so, just pick a type of course. It is worth studying the chart in the section below, in any case. It demonstrates which courses offer which settings.

Or you may feel spoilt for choice. In which case, completing the exercise outlined below may help.

Work out which type of course offers you the best settings

1. Study the chart in Figure 2.

2. Highlight the whole column which represents your preferred setting for working. If you have more than one preferred setting, highlight each one.

	Working alone	One-to-one	Small group	Larger group	On-line off-line	Phone	In your home	In tutor's home	In your office	Adult education centre	University centre	Score
Local authority classes				X								
Continuing education				X	(X)					X		
Business language courses	X	X	X		(X)	(X)						
Tailor-made courses	X	X	X		X	X					X	
Residential courses				X		X	X	X				
Home stay		X									(X)	
Going it alone	X											
Open university	X		X		X		X		X			

Fig. 2.   Which type of course offers the best setting for you?

3. With a different colour, highlight any others which you would also quite like.

4. Now work out a score for each row i.e. each sort of course. Award two points for each type of course where your first colour passes over a cross. Award one point for every cross which your second colour crosses. If the cross is in brackets, this means that that type of course does not always offer this setting. Therefore, only award half points.

5. Now turn your score into a mark out of five. Award five points for the three highest scoring. Award four for number four, three for number five, two for number six, one for number seven, none for number eight. Any which have scored zero automtically receive no marks.

Finding out which sort of course suits you

Enter the following scores in the table in Figure 3 in the following way.

1. Look at the descriptions of learning styles. Award a mark out of six to each type of course.

2. Look at the advantages. Give a score out of three to each type of course.

3. Look at the general descriptions. Award a mark out of three.

4. Fill in your setting score out of five.

Score	Learning style /6	Advantages /3	General description /3	Setting /5	Total /17	Disadvantage −3	Score out of 14
Local authority classes							
Continuing education							
Business language schools							
Tailor-made courses							
Residential courses							
Home stay							
Going it alone							
Open University							

Fig. 3. Which sort of course suits you?

5. Now add up your scores.

6. Study the disadvantages. Take a score out of three off what you have so far.

This should leave you with a score out of 14.

You should have now identified the best sort of course for you. Re-read the details for highest scoring type(s). Does that make sense? If more than one course has come out as the top scorer, use your own gut feeling to work out which one is best for you. Or could you combine two or three types of course? Could you do that anyway?

Now just look for one of those courses which has a good match with the content of your mind map.

Appendix 2 lists many addresses and web sites of courses. It is by no means comprehensive, and you should also conduct your own internet searches, consult your local library or local authority, and such publications as *Yellow Pages* or *Thomson Directory*. I have some personal experience of all of the ones I have listed.

THE STORY SO FAR

◆ You have decided why and what you want to learn.

◆ You have looked at your learning style.

◆ You have examined which sorts of course exist.

- ◆ You have decided in which settings you prefer to study.

- ◆ You have identified the best type of course for you.

- ◆ You have started to look for which course in your favourite type offers the most appropriate content.

3

Get organised

In this chapter you will:

◆ make decisions about what to buy to support your learning – dictionaries, grammar books, course books

◆ look at how to include work with multi-media equipment

◆ look at options about how to set out any written work

◆ establish a few good working practices.

By now, you have probably chosen and registered for your course. There is possibly a little while to go before you can start. You may be a little impatient. But if you have some time on your hands, you can spend some of it organising yourself for your course.

MATERIALS RECOMMENDED FOR YOUR COURSE

If you are studying at an adult education centre, a university continuing education centre or at a business language school, a course book will almost certainly be prescribed. The Open University sells you its own materials, and you really do need these. Residential courses tend to supply course books and materials as part of the package. If you are following a tailor-made course, you can really negotiate with your tutor about what sorts of materials are best.

As well as the actual book you are following, your teacher may recommend extra items, such as a dictionary or a grammar book. They may specify certain ones, or just recommend that you buy one. In any case, the suggestions below will help you decide which would be the best to buy for you.

Dictionaries

There is a lot of choice these days in what are called bi-lingual dictionaries. They have two sections to them, for example, French to English and English to French. They come in all sorts of different shapes and sizes, and it could take you a while to choose.

One thing to remember is that dictionaries go out of date very quickly. Our languages are changing all the time. I have an excellent German-English dictionary, revised in 1999, and produced by Oxford and Duden, respected publishers. And yet it does not contain the word for 'links' as in computer links. Always look carefully at the date of publication. Try to think of a new word and see whether the dictionary contains the word.

Many publishers are now producing bi-lingual dictionaries on CDs. You can install them on your computer. If you intend to do a lot of writing on your computer, these are excellent. Some even provide a spell-checker in the target language. However, if working with an 'inflected' language, i.e. a language which conveys meaning by putting endings on words, such as German, the computer will often not recognise the ending, and so the spell-check is not much use. One great advantage of CD dictionaries is that it is often possible to down-load up-dates, so you can really keep your dictionary current. One great disadvantage is that they won't slip into a back pocket or a handbag.

Size is important. If the dictionary is too small, after a few months it won't be much use to you. If you don't know the word, it won't be in the dictionary anyway. If it is too big, it will take a long time to use. I often recommend buying two to my students. One big one to stay on the desk at home or a dictionary on CD, and a smaller one. A good smaller one is the so-called school dictionary. It is adequate up to that all-important level of operational competence. They tend to be quite robust, because they are designed to be kept in school classrooms and used by up to 30 adolescents a day, and they will fit comfortably into a briefcase or a large handbag. If in addition you want something for when you're travelling light and doing the town or the shops, a conventional phrase book is your best bet. That really will fit into a back pocket.

Before you buy your dictionary, look at the print. So you do need to go to a shop. If the shop doesn't have the size you want, you can always buy via the internet later. The print must be of a size and clarity with which you feel comfortable. I was a fan of Collins' dictionaries for years. The word you look up is always in a very clear font and stands out from the page. Recently, other publishers have adopted this style.

And then . . . You must learn how to use your dictionary effectively. Which can sometimes mean not using it at all, but we'll deal with that later.

Remember, when choosing a dictionary consider:

◆ print

◆ size

◆ whether it is up to date

◆ whether you need more than one.

Grammar books

Grammar is a complex matter and many people fear it. We'll be taking the fear out of it in a later chapter. And the first step to getting rid of the fear is buying a grammar book. That reduces it to its component parts and is a prop to you in case you cannot remember it all.

However, there are just so many of them, and they do vary in detail. Look at my own *Selbstbedienung,* which is German grammar in a nutshell. It was designed for able students at the end of the third year at secondary school to work on independently. It starts with the items which are most likely to make a bigger difference to a grade at GCSE and works through until it has covered all areas of German grammar briefly. Compare that with Stopp's *Manual of German Grammar.* I bought that when I was still a student. It weighs a lot. I may have caused a bit of panic in Hudson's in Birmingham, as I put it in my bag and tried to see if I could still carry the bag, before I paid for the book.

If you're a beginner, or even if you're brushing up on languages you learnt at school, look out for anything with the words Key Stage 3 in the title or description. Like *Selbstbedienung*, these books, written for students only just beginning to understand grammar, will keep it clear and concise, with simple explanations. If you know everything in such a book, you could still perform well even beyond B1. I have used *Selbstbedienung* with AS students. Manuals like Stopp deal with subtleties and complications, and are fun to delve into – but only when you've mastered the basics.

Your dictionary will also have a thin grammar section. Once you know what is there, you can look certain points up very quickly. But these sections are never complete.

Your course book will also usually have a grammar section at the back. They tend, however, to only deal with the grammar points that the course book specifically teaches. This is useful when you are working through the book, but you do need a more complete picture of your language's grammar.

Again, you will need to visit a bookshop. Most internet sellers will allow you to return books, but that can make the process lengthy. You do need to check out which of the grammar books has the clearest layout for you.

Consider also whether you understand the explanations. Look in the contents for something you've never heard of. Turn to that page. Do you understand now? Don't worry about whether you'll remember, or that this is only one of many, many points. You only need to understand for the

moment. Don't worry even if you feel as I do about explanations to do with car engines or science. That you understand
now, but tomorrow you will be confused again. After all, you
are buying the book so that you can refer to it. You don't
have to remember. And eventually, after looking it up over
and over again, the point will stick. Believe me, it does.

So, in choosing a grammar book:

◆ go with your teacher's choice but check that it works for
   you

◆ go for a simple one to start with

◆ make sure the layout helps you to use it

◆ make sure you understand the explanations.

The course book

You may not have much choice in this either because it has
been prescribed by a teacher, or because you are studying a
more unusual language and there are only a few books.
Don't worry. Later, we shall be seeing how to get the most
out of your course book, no matter which strengths and
weaknesses it has.

But if you are studying one of the more popular languages –
French, German, Spanish or Italian – and you are following
a tailor-made course, you should give careful consideration
to your choice of book. Your tutor will probably still
recommend something, but it is worth asking them to pick
out three or four for you to choose from. Freelance teachers
should have several books, and most publishers will send

inspection copies for teachers to look at before they decide to buy.

Your ideal course book's content should match your mind map from Chapter 1 as much as possible, and also fit the time scale you have chosen. Does it also allow you to work in the settings you have chosen and does it fit your learning style?

Again, consider whether the layout and print suit you.

Does the book explain things well? Look at grammatical explanations in the text and in the grammar section at the back. Check also if there is a vocabulary list at the back of the book. It will be quicker to look things up from the book than using a dictionary.

Next look to see if the book suits you. Are the pictures of people like you or like the people you enjoy being with? Does it reflect your lifestyle?

Most importantly, look to see if the book *inspires* you. Do you look at the book and feel that you can't wait to get started? Can you see where you will be when you have finished the course?

If you are comparing several books, you could award each one marks out of five for the following. These questions are probably in order of importance, so if more than one book comes out well, look to see which has scored the most on the earlier questions.

◆ Does it inspire you?

◆ Does it cover your content?

◆ Does it fit your time scale?

◆ Does it allow you to work in your favourite settings?

◆ Does it reflect your learning style?

◆ Does the layout suit you?

◆ Does it explain grammar well?

◆ Is there a clear glossary at the back?

◆ Does it reflect your lifestyle?

USING MULTI-MEDIA EQUIPMENT

Using your personal computer (PC)

Even if you have decided to enrol for a more conventional course, your PC can really enhance your learning progress.

You may wish to supplement your course by buying a language learning CD. To some extent, it doesn't matter which one. Any of them bought from a reputable company are adequate, and in the end, French is French is French. Anything you do where you are listening and reading or even speaking and writing is going to be good practice. But if you are faced with a choice, do look at how well each one matches your mind map. And do check that the software is compatible with your hardware and operating system. A sound card is essential, and you might also consider whether you need speakers, a microphone and headphones.

Later, we shall also look at how you can use email and the internet for extending your learning.

There are also some authoring programs – such as Personal Tutor, where you enter lists of vocabulary and then the computer tests you. You do have to be careful that you enter the vocabulary accurately.

CD/cassette player/recorder

It is worth noting that your teacher or institution pays a lot for their CDs and cassettes. This is because they are also buying the right to use those materials throughout their institute. This includes permission to make copies for their students. That fact is often overlooked or even ignored because making copies is onerous. Push for it, though. If you can listen to the audio material in your own time, your listening ability can be greatly enhanced. Courses where the cost of the cassette or CD does not include the right to copy are a lot cheaper. *La Jolie Ronde*, French for children, sells its cassettes and CDs which last over a year for about £6.50, as compared with £45 or more for a set with other courses.

It is also worth using equipment on which you can record. You can use this for several purposes:

◆ recording parts of your lesson

◆ recording yourself and listening to yourself

◆ working with a native speaker (see Chapter 5)

◆ practising with another learner

◆ interviewing native speakers.

The very fact that you are recording your speech sharpens your effort.

However, don't rush out and buy a lot of new audio equipment. Make use of what you have for the moment. If you don't have your own, try to borrow some. Wait until you have been going a few weeks, so that you can work out what you really need.

Television and video equipment

A great way of learning is to watch television. This takes out some of the struggle of decoding the words as so much of it is visual. I remember once being very proud of myself because I had recorded *ET* in German. There is actually very little speech in that film. At least my students enjoyed themselves whilst they watched and they all remember how to ask if they can use the phone when they are on an exchange visit.

If you don't have access to television from the country whose language you are studying, you may be able to get your college or your 'learning partner' (see Chapter 5) to make some recordings for you.

Using a camcorder to film yourself and your classmates can be helpful too. You can see if your body language is matching what you are saying. Body language is an important part of communication, and is often different in different languages. You can also use your camcorder when you are visiting the country which speaks your new language. You will be recording sights and sounds which go together. This will greatly increase your understanding of the culture of that country. Understanding the culture enhances your language learning, just as understanding the language helps you to get to grips with the culture.

WHERE TO WRITE YOUR WORK

You will also need to think about how you are going to write your work down.

Work to be given in

One good idea for written homework is to word process it. Then, when your teacher has corrected it, you can do yourself a good copy. Keep the corrected one, or 'track changes' though. You always learn more from your mistakes than you do from what you get right.

If you are going to have to give work in, you will probably want to do that on paper, so if you do not intend to use your computer, you probably need a pad of A4 paper. Look for one which has margins, 80mm spaces and ready-punched holes.

Then you need to give some thought to where you store the corrected work. An A4 ring-binder is probably a good bet. But do you want to take it to and from college with you? Do you need a wallet folder, into which you can put completed work, corrected work and any hand-outs, which you can then sort out again when you get home? That at least will force you to look at them again.

Hand-outs

Teachers will often use hand-outs. Would it be an idea to have a separate folder for them? Perhaps you would like to divide that up into administrative items, reading practice, speaking practice, listening practice, writing practice, grammar and information about the country or countries where your language is used. Have a few more file dividers in case some other categories emerge as you go along.

Vocabulary

You will need a space for writing down vocabulary. A good tip is to have a note book which will fit in a pocket or a handbag. Then you can have it with you all the time, so that you can learn vocabulary anywhere. And if you're in the country which speaks your language, you can write down new words. A5 hardback with 80mm spaced lines is a good start, but you might like to look ahead at Chapter 4, before you decide finally on a note book. Or perhaps you'll want to get two . . .

Mind maps

These are an excellent way of writing down what you have learnt. You will need plain paper for this (ready punched) and perhaps a variety of coloured pens. Those jelly pens are good to work with, or some nice rollerballs or fineliners. Something which you can enjoy, in any case. Again, you will need a folder to keep your mind maps in.

File cards

Some people find it useful to buy small filing cards and filing boxes, especially when it comes to revising for exams. They can carry a few cards around with them, and look at them while they are waiting for the bus.

Small bits of card and blutak

Other people are happy to plaster their homes with vocabulary. They have cards all over the house, sometimes colour-coded for different areas of knowledge. Do you remember when the children were small and you perhaps did something similar with their spellings and tables? Well, now it's your turn!

Writing equipment

You will certainly need at least one pen, but think about getting a variety of colours. A pencil and rubber will also be important, and therefore also a pencil sharpener.

NOW TRY THIS

Don't go too mad buying a lot of stationery. You may find you want different things as you go along, or one way of recording your work suits you better than another. Nevertheless, go through the above again, make yourself a shopping list and go to a good stationery store like Staples. Take this book with you and let it and the store inspire you.

When you get home again, unpack everything carefully, and label it ready. Imagine yourself using those items in a few days. Find a place where you are going to store them. Make sure it is somewhere where you can pick them up easily. You are ready to go!

FROM DAY 1

Here are a few ideas you can use from your very first lesson.

Writing down vocabulary

Fold the pages of your book into two or four, depending on how big it is. Write the words in the foreign language in the left column, the English meaning on the right. Don't worry about writing down every new word you meet. Perhaps concentrate on the ones which are going to be most useful to you.

Learning vocabulary

First work from the foreign language to English. Cover up the English column. Test yourself. Put a pencil cross by each word you didn't know. When you have gone through one page, test yourself on the ones marked with a cross. Rub out the cross if you have it right this time. When you know all of the words from foreign language to English, go back and test yourself from English to foreign language. When that page is complete go to the next page. After the second page is complete, go back and do the first again. Later, as the book gets fuller, you should complete the current page, the page before and then an earlier page, randomly chosen.

Making mind maps

After each lesson, try to make a mind map or add to one you have already started. You should put the theme in the middle, e.g. 'Shopping' (better still to put your word in the foreign language), and then the first set of branches could be about the transactions you have learnt to do. Next come the particular phrases you have used, followed by items/lists of vocabulary. You may not be able to write a full list here, but that could be in your vocabulary book, so you'll be working on it anyway. You may like to use different colours for different levels or different branches. Reserve red for later, though.

You can test yourself by trying to reproduce the mind map. When you check, put in any bits you had forgotten in red. Next time you revise from that mind map, your weaker areas will show up in red.

Use recordings

Record yourself, if possible with a class mate, using the language you have met in the lesson. Be critical of yourself – you may have a good giggle at first, as well. But that does no harm.

Listen to any material you met in the lesson. It will become easier the more you listen to it. Eventually you will know it off by heart.

Make friends with your course book

No matter how good or bad your text book is, if, by the time you come to the end of it, you know its contents off by heart, you will know a lot of your chosen language. Be familiar with how it works. Do they use special symbols to show which are reading or listening exercises? Do they have grammar points in special boxes? What is contained in the grammar section at the back of the book? How useful is the glossary? Do you know all of the words in the glossary?

If your text book becomes a little battered, be happy. It shows you are making good use of it. And you can start the process of beginning to get to know your text book even before you start the course.

THE STORY SO FAR

◆ You have chosen a course.

◆ You have bought your dictionary, course book and grammar book.

◆ You have given some consideration to multi-media equipment.

◆ You have given some thought to how you will organise your written work.

◆ You have equipped yourself for your first lesson.

◆ You know how to make best use of the first few lessons.

$$\textcircled{4}$$

Develop the Magpie Instinct

In this chapter you will:

◆ learn how to 'collect' language

◆ learn what sort of language to collect

◆ look at where to find that language

◆ find out how to make use of the language you have found

◆ really begin to have fun with your chosen language.

REAL MAGPIES

I would call my German friend, Gabi, a magpie. We have arranged many exchanges over the years between our respective schools. There comes a point in the day, when you're on a exchange visit, when all the problems have been solved, the next day is sorted out and you can relax.

'Is it time to get the sherry out, Gill?' she asks.

And whilst I go and organise the sherry, she goes and gets her notebook and pen.

'Now Gill,' she starts as soon as we are sitting relaxed with the drinks. 'You said something today about "You don't have to be a rocket scientist to see that it was the lights not working which made the bus late." Did I get that right?'

I confirm the new expression and she writes it down. Then she tries it out on me a few times, using slightly different examples. When she is satisfied she has it right, she closes her book, folds her arms contentedly and concentrates on her sherry.

At some point in the next few days, I will see her pause, look at me mischievously and say something like 'You don't have to be a rocket scientist to see that if they don't all turn up on time, the bus will be late setting off.'

Like the magpie, Gabi has seen something she likes and put it in a place she knows it will be safe. But she makes it even more her own by using it as soon as possible.

You need to start collecting language. That doesn't mean making long lists, though. I have seen many, many students laboriously copy down reams of vocabulary – perhaps never to be looked at again. Even if they do refer to them when they go to write the essay for homework, or when they revise for the exam, I doubt whether they retain many of the phrases for very long. The point is:

◆ You need to collect language which appeals to you, which gives you a bit of fun and which you know you can use.

◆ And you have to use it fairly soon after you have collected it. Putting the language somewhere and using it actively fixes it in your mind.

Gabi is obviously already a fluent speaker. But you don't have to wait until you are to start collecting. One of my students, Gordon, is a businessman who has to learn German because the head office of his firm is in Switzerland. He is definitely not a linguist. He has difficulty getting his mouth around some of the words. He does not understand grammar. His Swiss colleagues barely give him the chance to practise his German because they want to try out their already excellent English. Yet he still manages to impress them from time to time.

We have been using a text book. In some ways it is a rather dry and uninteresting one. But every few pages there are some cartoons illustrating idiomatic phrases. We have a bee in our bonnet, but the Germans have a bird; when they are hungover they have a tomcat; and our noses get put out of joint, but the Germans have their ties (that's right, their ties not their toes) trodden on.

Every time we come to one of these pages, my client makes a note of the phrase which appeals to him most, and within a day or two tries it out on one of his colleagues in Switzerland. He complains to his boss that people who work for a certain firm are always adding their mustard to the matter in hand. We would more normally complain about them putting their oar in. His boss laughs, congratulates him on the excellent progress he is making with his German and Gordon feels more confident. Making people laugh when you have only just started to speak their language is an achievement. Again, he has found something that appeals to him, made a note and made himself use it.

WHERE TO KEEP YOUR PET WORDS

How people might collect language has to be an individual choice. You may have already made decisions after working through Chapter 3 about where you might want to store new expressions. Is that working for you at the moment?

Or what about the following?

◆ Gabi uses 15cm x 20cm hardback note book. It is thick because it contains 250 pages of good quality paper. She prefers unlined, and she writes with a good pen. She often buys herself such a note book from a favourite museum here in England. When each one is full, she has something of beauty, which is pleasant to leaf through.

◆ One student keeps his pet phrases on computer file. He scrolls them round, making an effort to use each one in turn. He deletes them when he feels that he knows them. He never works with more than 20 at a time.

◆ I myself have an all-purpose note book. It is a little more utilitarian than Gabi's. Odd phrases for the languages I study are mixed in with my ideas for books and articles. When I'm waiting somewhere, I'm either adding to my notes or reading through them. If I want to write a letter or phone a friend, I have a look through first. And when a book is full, I look through again before putting it safely on a bookshelf. It is still taken down every so often.

◆ Some students put phrases on the walls or the fridge.

◆ My daughter wrote phrases on filing cards and carried them around in her back pocket when she was studying for her GCSEs.

Remember, note books come in all sorts of shapes and sizes. Do you want something which fits a briefcase, a wallet, a handbag or a pocket? Do you want to use your computer? Do you want something for when you are working at a desk in a building, or something which you can carry around with you? Do you want something which suits both purposes or a different one for each?

Whatever you decide, you can change your mind again. Be flexible. But make sure you are acting like a magpie – find what you like, put it away safely, use it.

WHAT YOU MIGHT COLLECT

Rule number one is you collect what is relevant to you. This might be:

◆ Specialist words and phrases to do with your work.

◆ Specialist words and phrases to do with your hobby.

◆ Specialist phrases to do with the work, hobbies and appearance of friends and family.

◆ Words and phrases which amuse you (as Gordon does).

- Words which fill gaps you are aware of (e.g. your course may have taught you all the normal colours, but you might come across the word for avocado, which just happens to be the colour of your bathroom suite).

- Useful little gems which might help you with everyday transactions – probably ones which you don't remember coming across in your course (e.g. 'Do you think you could . . .').

- More sophisticated expressions (as Gabi does).

- Phrases which help you to structure the language (e.g. I can, you can, he can etc.).

- Words which might shock mildly (rat poison, dustbin – these words were a great favourite of my best friend at school).

- Words and phrases which are to do with a situation you might be facing shortly (if you're going camping soon, look through language about camp-sites and try to learn some key phrases).

- Words and phrases which are so new that they haven't made it to your bilingual dictionary yet (e.g. when a new craze hits like bungee jumping did a few years ago I had the French expression in my note book several months before it appeared in a dictionary).

WHERE TO FIND THE LANGUAGE

It is actually all around you, even if you are not in the country which speaks the language you are studying. In fact, you can collect language from anything you read or hear.

Sometimes, though, you may not have realised where the opportunities exist for reading and hearing your new language.

Look out for words of interest in the following places.

From home

◆ your course book

◆ your teacher

◆ in the dictionary when you are looking for something else

◆ magazines you may be able to find

◆ off the internet

◆ from your contact with a native speaker – a work colleague, a penfriend or e-mail friend

◆ foreign radio

◆ foreign television

◆ the instructions for cooking pasta or making your microwave work

◆ songs – either authentic ones from the country whose language you are studying, or those created as part of a course.

When you're in the country where your language is spoken

◆ all of the above, still, and more intensely

- conversations you overhear on the bus, in the shop, in the café

- road signs

- ads in shop windows

- flyers and advertising left on your car or in your supermarket trolley or put through your letterbox

- junk mail

- menus.

A WORD OF WARNING

You could get really carried away and try to collect all of these types of phrases in all of these types of situation. That could at some point seem all too much, you could become totally overwhelmed, and be left with the feeling that your chosen language contains just too many phrases and you could never have a hope of learning them. You have to retain the fun in this one. And that means taking that phrase, which is all yours, and showing it off to somebody who's going to listen. You're saying, 'Hey folks look what I can do!' So just a few at a time is better.

HOW THIS WORKS

Babies acquire their language by constantly listening and imitating the patterns of words around them. They come to understand the words they hear and begin to use the phrases they need with increasing competence. But this doesn't work so well with our second language because:

◆ our first language constantly takes up more space than the new one

◆ our need is not as great

◆ we're unlikely to have the same amount of exposure to the second language as we did to the first.

Even if we go and live in the country where our language is spoken, we still tend to think and dream in our own language – and possibly even read or watch TV – and we may still be living amongst people who speak our native tongue. Indeed, there are many expatriates who never master the language of their new homeland and often it has not been because of unwillingness on their part. They have just not found the right tool.

Just like the baby, though, we learn to understand many times more phrases than we can actually produce. Eventually, after a lot of time and practice, we are able to use this passive store of language actively. By becoming a proactive magpie, we're getting our hand a bit more on the tool and accelerating that process.

And there are other things you can do too. Read on.

Try this
For a whole week 'collect' a phrase a day. Make an effort to use it within two days of finding it. How do you feel at the end of the week? Is your confidence growing? How are others reacting to your new language?

In the long-term

◆ Try to gather and try out at least two or three phrases a week.

◆ Experiment with the best way to store your gems – a small note book, a larger one, the computer?

◆ Tell someone else what you're doing and ask them to check from time to time if you're still doing it.

THE STORY SO FAR

◆ You are following your carefully chosen course, you are fully equipped for that course and are already putting a few good habits into practice.

◆ You have started to seek the language proactively.

◆ You are storing the language in a place which suits you and is easy for you to retrieve.

◆ You are putting your new words and phrases into practice.

◆ You are having some fun with your new language.

5

Go Native

In this chapter you will:

◆ explore the possibilities of working with a native speaker of your chosen language

◆ look at the advantages of going on an exchange visit

◆ look at how you can make the most of your friendship

◆ find out how to make contact with a native speaker.

STRETCHING OUT THE HAND OF FRIENDSHIP

Picture this. A group of you go to the theatre together. You watch a performance of *Under Milkwood* in French. What it loses in the translation it makes up for in the acting. You and your friends have a meal together, return to the home of one of the others to discuss it further and then you put the world right. You speak French because you are in France. But occasionally you use English or German, because the group is made up of French people who speak English and German, Germans who speak English and French and English people who speak French and German. Sometimes you use your own language because you can't quite manage the French. Sometimes, though, you use English or German because a phrase which only exists in that language expresses better what you want to say. And you all understand each other. The hand of friendship has been fully stretched.

That happened to me when I was a student.

Perhaps I am a little naïve in thinking that if more people spoke foreign languages there would be less possibility of war. But I certainly would not be able to tolerate war between my own country and that of one of my very good friends whom I have come to know through learning their language. It actually hurts physically when I confront the continued hatred felt by some towards the Germans brought forward from the first and second world wars. Their strong feelings are about the parents and grandparents of the Germans to whom I have become very close.

Take a good look at your mind map. Look for the bottom line, perhaps something that isn't even written down there. What is the real underlying motive behind your desire to learn a foreign language? It will be at least to do with effective communication and at best condoning deep friendship. Effective communication, in any case, depends on a willingness to find out what motivates the other, and that involves dropping any concerns and considerations about the differences between you. What you get as a replacement is understanding and appreciation, and these are a form of friendship.

So, you either start with friendship as your main motivation, or you obtain friendship though your desire to communicate. That's the bigger picture.

THE ADVANTAGES OF CONTACT WITH A NATIVE SPEAKER

Of course, it will be a while before you can discuss *Under Milkwood* or put the world right. But you can start working with a native speaker straight away.

Working with a native speaker of your chosen language offers many advantages.

◆ You will constantly be presented with an accurate pattern of language.

◆ You will probably be matched with someone who has similar interests to yourself, so will be able to work specifically on the most appropriate area of vocabulary for you.

◆ You could make a new life-long friend.

AN EXCHANGE VISIT

Perhaps the most important part of my work as a full-time teacher was organising exchange visits for my pupils. I hardly needed to teach then after we came home. They just lapped up new language. And they always came back with much more than they had before. They continued to organise their own exchanges. How delightful it was for me to walk along the main shopping street in Cologne and bump into a pupil I had taken out there on an exchange visit two years earlier. She and her German partner were so engrossed in chatting away in German that they didn't see me at first. Then there was the pupil from my tutor group, a rather awkward child, whom I had persuaded to take part in the French exchange.

She and her partner spent hours literally exchanging vocabulary and writing it down in books. Their magpie instinct was in overdrive. The icing on the cake came as, at the end of our visit to France, the French mum claimed Julie to be absolutely charming. She would be welcome again any time. Nobody had ever said that about Julie before. And she did go back. For all four girls the language was not the main point any more.

When you go on an exchange visit, you stay in the home of a family who speaks your new language. At some point, a member or members of their family visit you. For school children, this lasts one to two weeks. For adults, it is sometimes shorter. Whilst you are there, you are totally surrounded by the language. You acquire much more and you increase your ability to make the most of what you do have. One of my pupils, one of these people who speak at a hundred miles an hour, began to speak as fast in German as she did in English. She even managed to get her word order and her endings right.

You also learn about the culture of the country and find out about habits and rituals which are different from our own, which makes you look more closely at your own. Isn't it fascinating that a French family I know often have two desserts on a Sunday, and invite the elderly widow next door to share the second one? Isn't the German habit of having cake with coffee in the afternoon civilised? And what about that game the English play, where the team that's in goes out until they're out, then they come in again? You may have known before you went that some of these things existed. But while you're there, you begin to appreciate why.

So, gradually, it stops being them and us, and starts being just us. Language becomes a means to an end rather than an end in itself. You become so highly motivated that what had seemed a difficulty becomes insignificant, just a blip. You just want to find out more and more about this alternative way of living, and mastering the language is a step in the right direction. As the layers are peeled back, you become more surprised by the similarities between you than the differences. Because you understand the differences.

You become aware of which items of language you need to know in order to function in this new relationship. And you might consider using a native speaker learning partner as a way of acquiring that language.

GET YOURSELF A LEARNING PARTNER

This is an extension of what has happened for years between penfriends who are learning each other's language. People send each other letters, often in their own language, and the learner is presented with an accurate structure which they can adapt to suit their own needs. Occasionally, they will send a reply in their target language, but the recipient will not usually correct any mistakes in this. E-mail has already speeded up this process and makes replies more immediate and news more current. Woking with a learning partner fine-tunes this process.

The partners choose topics they wish to learn more about. They communicate in their own language, so that a good pattern of the foreign language is presented. They also communicate in the foreign language, so that their partner can correct their work and give them extra useful phrases. They can both choose topics which suit them. It works well if both partners are working at about the same level, though two beginners together can cause problems and may need extra help from their teachers, especially when they are negotiating what to do. Students of differing levels can also work together, as long as topics are carefully selected.

This works best if:

◆ each partner is prepared to make the same amount of effort

◆ each partner is responsible for their own learning

◆ each partner states how and what they want to learn

◆ 50% is completed in each language, and 50% of the time one is using one's native language.

The possible settings for working with a learning partner are:

◆ e-mail and snailmail

◆ telephone

◆ video conferencing

◆ via a chat room

◆ exchange of audio and video tapes

◆ one-to-one, face-to-face (possibly as part of an exchange visit).

Here are few ides for topics you could use:

◆ introducing yourself

◆ talking about your family

◆ talking about your home/area where you live

◆ talking about your work

◆ talking about your hobbies

◆ discussing an item of news

◆ discussing your hopes for the future

◆ role-playing a shopping or restaurant situation

◆ role-playing a work situation – e.g. chasing an order, making a complaint, obtaining information.

FINDING A PARTNER

Even for adults, it is best to find a partner through an organisation you know. It is, of course, much easier for the commonly taught European languages, but possible also for almost any language. Consider the following.

Twin town

Many towns have partners in France or Germany, and even Belgium, Spain and Italy. Your twinning organisation will often arrange short trips to and from that town, and this is an ideal opportunity to get to know a native speaker. You can even request to be put in touch with someone who has similar interests.

Your teacher

Your teacher probably has a wealth of contacts in appropriate countries. Ask them if they can put you in contact with someone.

The Central Bureau for Cultural Exchanges and Visits

This has always been the main organisation for putting schools together for exchanges. However, the need for life-long learning is acknowledged everywhere now, and they will respond to approaches from adults. They do tend to work more with whole groups: you could always get your class to apply on mass.

Organisations connected with your work and hobbies

The firm which you work for or the club you belong to may have international contacts and could put you in touch with a like-minded individual. If not, an internet search will certainly find a company similar to your own or an organisation for people with similar hobbies to your own. We do have the advantage that most other nationalities are very keen to improve their English, so finding a learning partner should not be difficult.

NOW TRY THIS

◆ Find yourself a partner.

◆ Decide on the settings you want to use.

◆ Make yourself a list of topics you would like to try (perhaps some of the items from your gaps which your course does not supply?).

◆ Start negotiations (remember the 50% rule).

◆ Have a go at your first topic.

THE STORY SO FAR

◆ You have started your course, for which you are well equipped, and have started putting a few good habits into practice.

◆ You have found a learning partner.

◆ You have decided on some topics and settings you would like to try.

◆ You have negotiated what and how to learn.

◆ You have tried out your first tandem session.

6

Talk the Hind Leg Off a Donkey – in Any Language

In this chapter you will:

◆ take a closer look at communication

◆ learn to make the most of what you know

◆ look at opportunities for practising

◆ find out how to obtain more patterns of language – without major effort

◆ get even more fun out of your language learning

◆ discover what to do when your perfectly presented phrase or sentence is answered with a torrent of words you can't understand easily.

COMMUNICATION

We are talking about talking, the most basic form of communication. Even the cats which wail at night are doing just that, though in a far less sophisticated way than we humans. Talking is a mixture of listening and speaking. One person speaks, the other listens, then responds in speech. Effective communication happens when speaker and listener create the same pictures in their heads. For this to happen the listener really tunes in to what is being said, and the speaker chooses their language carefully.

This does not necessarily mean merely using beautifully constructed sentences. After all, which communicates the best:

◆ A struggling 'Excuse me please sir, could you possibly tell me whether you have any . . . ?'

◆ Or a confident 'Any cheesecake?' as the waiter comes to your table for the dessert order and you smile at them?

The use of body language and finding the key word communicates much better than the highly structured, polished, rehearsed phrase. The Spanish use this superbly. They cope with their tourist industry by just knowing a few key words in major European languages and leave the rest to their imaginative use of gesture and facial expression.

MAKE THE MOST OF WHAT YOU KNOW

I once attended a workshop for people who have to do presentations. The point was made that we often use too many words. We were given an exercise where we were limited to communicating in five words. A group of us had to perform a task together, and we were given our five words by another group. We had to move a pile of bricks from one part of the garden to another. Well, we stuck to our five words and were able to communicate enough to get the job done. We even managed to chat about whether worms and the fruit on a bush in the garden were edible. (One of our words was 'food'.) The main point was that we were willing to use what little we had to communicate.

You may not be very long into your course yet, but I am sure you already have more than five words in your chosen language. So how much more could you do?

I explained about the exercise with the five words and the pile of bricks to my second-year French class. I asked them to talk in groups of three about what they did on their holidays last year and what they were going to do next summer. They bought into the game. The number one ground rule was that they should not attempt to use anything they didn't know. Number two was that they should try to use everything that they did know. I was delighted that they all managed to keep going for the 20 minutes. They enjoyed the exercise. We did a debrief in English afterwards, and it was clear that there had been very few misunderstandings.

PRACTISING

We succeeded with our pile of bricks and my second-year students succeeded because they were willing to have a go. They took part. That is what made the practice effective.

I used to be a visiting oral examiner for German, and in recent years have had to conduct the oral exam for my own GCSE pupils. I have frequently noticed that although two candidates may have produced exactly the same language, one has communicated better than the other. They would probably have been effective in the real-life situation. Even some candidates who produced language with more errors in it communicated more effectively. They made the roles they were playing and the conversations they were having real. I always wished I could award extra marks for the attitude which was making the language work better.

Can you bring this into your practice?

What about working with a partner in class, and even getting together out of class for extra sessions? If you're working one-to-one with a tutor, or on the phone, perhaps you could ask your tutor to give you more opportunities to try this out. And this is a great opportunity to work with your learning partner. You could use the following contexts.

◆ anything which has come up in your course for oral practice

◆ shopping

◆ dealing with lost property

◆ restaurants and cafés

◆ finding your way around

◆ dealing with the police and reporting accidents

◆ making complaints

◆ finding out about hotels and tourist attractions

◆ dealing with the car

- talking about yourself, your family and friends

- talking about your work

- talking about your hopes for the future

- talking about your hobbies and interests

- talking about your holidays.

Practising methodically

It was often my experience when working with teenagers that I would give them a pair activity, and two minutes later they would cry 'Finished miss!'. Well of course, they hadn't. They wouldn't be finished until they could do that conversation upside down in their sleep and they would remember it forever. They were actually bored with it.

So, how do you stop yourself getting bored before that conversation and similar ones are etched on your brain? Try this, for example, on a conversation which might take place in a shop.

1. Do the conversation as is – i.e. just read the printed version out of the book.
2. Change roles.
3. Add more expression.
4. Add different attitudes and emotions. Either of you or both could be bored, happy, impatient, sad, excited, afraid, polite, rude, silly, business-like – you can think of others.
5. Vary the pace and pitch. Speak quickly, slowly, loudly, or quietly.
6. 'Walk' the conversation. Act it out. You might be

beginning to feel a bit silly, but better now than when you do it in real life.

7. Record your conversation. It will sharpen your 'performance' and also give you a chance to assess yourself. You'll soon get used to hearing your own voice.

8. Alter bits of it – nothing too complicated, though, if you're working with a class mate. Maybe you could ask for 2 kilos instead of 3, or for chocolate instead of soap powder, and maybe you could change the prices and the change given – numbers always need a lot of practice anyway.

9. If you are working one-to-one with a teacher or with your native speaker, ask them to include a surprise. Maybe there are no more apples. Or perhaps there is suddenly a fire in the shop and you have to run out. This is good rehearsal for the surprises which come in real life (though they are usually linguistic rather than dramatic) and can give you some new language to experience.

Working on the phone

A major feature of learning by phone is the conversation or speech you have to prepare for each lesson. Further practice includes:

1. Going over the speech or role play with your teacher. They take the other role if appropriate.

2. They correct you if you make mistakes and give you new phrases as needed.

3. You are given about five phrases to rehearse for the next lesson. These will be ones you were less confident about and ones which will be useful for next week's topic.

4. You try to learn these phrases and use them actively,

perhaps in your contact with native speakers before your next lesson.

OBTAINING NEW PATTERNS OF LANGUAGE FOR FREE

When you work one-to-one with a tutor, perhaps on the phone, when you work with your learning, and when you are in a 'real' situation, you can still carry on improving your spoken language, if you keep your wits about you and your ears open.

Remember the magpie instinct you started developing in Chapter 4? This is where you can make some really good use of it. Don't be too ambitious though, or you will get swamped. If, in each 'natural' conversation you hold, you can acquire one new pattern or piece of vocabulary, you will continue to make rapid progress.

Listen consciously, taking account of the form of the phrases, as your partner speaks.

'Would you like to go to the shops or would you rather stay in and watch the football?' says your partner.

Now, you know 'play football' but not 'stay in and watch the football'. The 'stay in and . . .' appeals to you (not *just* because you would like to watch the football). So you confirm it by reflecting back.

'Mm. I think I'd like to stay in and watch the football,' you reply.

You internalise the phrase, maybe adding it to your collection in your note book.

A little later you use the language as your own.

'Shall we go to the pub?' you say to your partner, 'or would you rather stay in and watch a video?'

You're actually doing what you did with your own language when you were a baby. But because you haven't got so long to do it, you make a more conscious effort.

GETTING EVEN MORE FUN OUT OF LEARNING YOUR FOREIGN LANGUAGE

Hopefully, everything I have suggested so far is working for you, and you are enjoying learning your new language because you are being successful. Hopefully, too, you are losing all inhibition and really getting into practising conversations with your partner.

But it is also important to remember that language is power. When negotiating partners share a language, they have equal power. When you lack the language of the country in which you try to transact, you have less power. Surely, you may be saying, if the native speaker has more command of the language, they have more power? This is to some extent true, but only as far as you let that be the case. If you refuse to be put off by the greater sophistication of what they are using, and you insist on speaking their language even though they speak yours better – we English do have a problem here, as everyone else is so keen to practise on us –

you actually more than make up for the power that you have lost.

Now, when you are aware of what is happening, you can really have some fun. It is a matter of confidence and determination. Which brings us to the next point.

HOW TO COPE WITH THE TORRENTS

What do you do when your carefully chosen and beautifully rehearsed phrase so impresses a native speaker that they come back at you in a torrent of language you can make no sense of?

This happened to me when I went to France for the first time. I already had a good O-level and A-level in French. I spoke it perfectly, I thought, and had enjoyed chatting away to the French assistant at school. But after I asked for a cheese sandwich in impeccable French, the waiter asked me lots of complicated questions in a language I'd never heard before. On the other hand, I have for many years taken pupils in the second year of French to France for the day, and they have found their way around town, reading French instructions and asking people the way, they have gone shopping in French and ordered food and drink in French at the café. A year later they have gone on their first French exchange visit and functioned perfectly well in families which have very little English. They were seldom fazed. So, what's the difference?

They have been taught how to cope and what to expect!

This is the drill.

◆ Expect the torrent.

◆ Anticipate before it comes what might be included in there. For example, if you are ordering an ice-cream, they may ask you what size or flavour you want, and what sort of toppings.

◆ Watch and understand the speaker's body language. (Body language differs a little from country to country – ask your teacher to include this in your lessons.)

◆ Listen carefully for those key words. You may even need to use some in your reply – in the case of the ice-cream, maybe *medium, vanilla* and *chocolate sauce*.

◆ If you still do not understand, have 'Please can you speak more slowly?' or 'Could you repeat that please?' ready. (Never, of course, 'Do you speak English?') Most people will naturally simplify or speak more slowly if they see you are making an effort.

◆ If they do insist on speaking English, reply again in your chosen language, possibly adding, 'Thank you for trying to help me, but I really do want to practise my . . . So could we continue in . . . ?'

Have fun!

THE STORY SO FAR

◆ You have carefully chosen your course, for which you are well equipped and well organised. You are developing good working practices, including working with native speakers. You are collecting language.

◆ You are making the most of the language you already know.

◆ You are using an effective method for practising language you meet.

◆ You using talking as a means of discovering new patterns of language.

◆ You are getting even more fun out of using your chosen language.

◆ You are learning how to cope when native speakers assume you know more than you do.

7

Completing the Jigsaw Puzzle

In this chapter we shall look at:

◆ the uses and nature of reading in a foreign language

◆ extensive reading

◆ reading for gist

◆ intensive reading

◆ reading as a tool for learning

◆ how to obtain reading materials, many of them free of charge.

THE PURPOSE OF READING

Language study is frequently divided into four skills – listening, reading, speaking and writing. In the last chapter we looked at talking, which combines listening and speaking. There is the other sort of listening where you don't respond in speech e.g. station announcements, listening tests on your course, radio etc. The Bavarian education department describes language learning targets and levels in very similar terms to our own National Curriculum and the European Passport, but adds the target of understanding and using gesture and body language. In any case, reading is clearly a skill in its own right.

Reading is also the means of acquiring new language. Even at the very beginning of your course, and especially if you have started to develop the magpie instinct quite well, reading is one your most useful tools. Certainly, by the time you reach that all-important level of operational competence, if you're aiming for a B or above at GCSE or you want to progress beyond National Curriculum Level 5 (out of 8), then an extensive programme of reading in the foreign language is one of the keys to making further progress rapidly.

Many experts on language tuition argue that we acquire our knowledge through listening. This reflects how we learn our mother tongue, and is therefore very natural. However, it has been my experience that adult learners prefer to have everything in writing. I would include myself in this also. I would even go as far as to say that learners aged 12 and above need the prop of the written word. The whole education system so far has taught the importance of the print form and written word. We have been conditioned to rely on it.

EXTENSIVE READING
This means reading a lot, but not being too worried about understanding every single word. We cannot hope to read as accurately in the foreign language as we do in our own. But we can still get enough understanding from what we read.

Today, I was reading a French novel written for adults. I probably understood 95% of the words, and much of what was left was still understandable, because it was a bit like looking at a jigsaw puzzle which had a few pieces missing. The surrounding pieces suggested what was on the missing ones. Also, I was reading some French words which I understood but which I would not be able to produce. Read them often enough and you will be able to produce them. So this can be a process which you never have to give up. Sometimes I pick up a book which is a bit harder to read. But so that reading still remains a pleasure rather than a chore, I limit myself to looking up just three words on each page. It is enough to enable gist understanding.

Even at the very beginning of your study, you can develop the habit of flicking through a magazine or newspaper, or having a look at a few web sites. Be content if you are just understanding two or three bits of information at this stage. Notice when you begin to understand more. You will recognise which is the weather forecast, the football results, the word for goal keeper, the TV guide, what the click-on buttons on the web site mean, because there is a certain visuality of the text which is familiar to you. Maybe we've only got a few edge pieces of the puzzle at the moment, but it's a start and already we have an idea of what the bigger picture will be. Incidentally, I have found that adults are actually much better at this than younger learners. They have more life experience to go on. And don't forget to jot down just one phrase in your notebook.

INTENSIVE READING

There will be times, however, when you need to understand a text in more detail. Perhaps you have to interpret a document for work, for homework or as a test or exam, or it's simply that you want to understand every word and get more of a hold on how your chosen language works. Try this:

1. If you possibly can, have your text in a form in which you can write on it. Blow it up if you can, and if it is word-processed and you have it in electronic form, double space it, but print a hard copy to work on.

2. Read your text three times. You will find you understand much more after the third reading than the first, but it won't improve so much after a fourth or subsequent reading. Three is an optimum number. Actually, if you just carried on reading it over and over, you would eventually understand it all. Your brain is a brilliant de-coding computer. I was on holiday in Malta recently, and kept reading the back of the milk carton, where the Maltese obviously said something different from the English. It was set out differently and had far more words. On the last day of the holiday it clicked. I read it out to my husband in what I thought was Maltese pronunciation. It was telling us how much protein and calcium etc was contained in the milk.

3. Now take a pencil and write in each word you know because you have met it before or that you recognise because it sounds a bit like English (or any other language you know for that matter) – reading out aloud is useful here.

4. Look at each sentence individually. You may have the meaning of the sentence without understanding every

word. Your brain has arced over and completed the jigsaw puzzle.

5. For those sentences you still do not understand, look for the key words. They are probably nouns (naming words), verbs (doing words) or expressions of time or place. A little more intensive study here may make the meaning apparent. It's detective work.

6. If there are still gaps, particularly in key words, now and only now, use your dictionary. Underline the word you are looking up – it will help you to find it again in the text.

7. If the sentence still does not make sense or that sentence seems to contradict the whole, have a look at some of the smaller words. Amazing what difference *not, never, although, but, despite* and many other such words can make to meaning. These types of devices are frequently used in exams to catch candidates out. Full of nasty tricks, linguists. But those same words also enrich our languages, and are therefore important in any case.

FINDING READING MATERIALS

There are many sources of reading materials, many of them free. Look at the list below. The ones marked with * won't cost you anything more than time and effort. If they are marked (*), they will be free of charge most of the time. Try to do some extra reading each week, or better still, every day.

◆ * The Internet. One great advantage of working on web sites is that you learn a lot of vocabulary unconsciously from recognising the function of buttons without knowing the words in advance. Use search engines to find information about topics in your chosen language. Some language sites have been included in Appendix 5.

◆ * Multi-lingual packaging. You know, the instructions which come with your new electric kettle. However, beware of bad translations. Only look at the language if it matches the country of origin of the product. You do have the advantage of a gist translation into your own language. These make excellent texts for intensive work.

◆ * Junk mail or advertising left on your car or picked up at the shops when you are abroad. You will understand much of this quite easily because you recognise the form.

◆ (*) What your learning partner writes to you. You could even ask them to send you extra materials in your areas of interest.

◆ Reading schemes for learners of your chosen language. These reflect your level of ability in reading but not your interests. Unfortunately, these are not always produced for adults. Some are listed in Appendix 3.

◆ Reading schemes for young readers in your chosen language. Again, these may be a little childish in content, but they will provide you with simpler but still authentic texts.

◆ Reading schemes in your chosen language for adult native speakers who are learning to read. These are ideal, as they will be a stepping stone to more complex texts and will be of interest to any age group.

◆ (*) Manuals to do with your work produced for the countries which speak your chosen language.

◆ Texts in your course book. (Perhaps you could read intensively those texts which were meant for extensive reading.)

◆ Subscription magazines. These come at all levels and may be produced monthly or termly. Sometimes, a university continuing education centre or adult education centre will stock a few. Some examples are listed in Appendix 3. If you are in a class, ask your teacher to organise a bulk purchase of these – discounts are often given.

◆ Many university continuing education departments have access to the main language departments at the university which will have their own bank of resources. Find out how to use these.

Have fun reading!

THE STORY SO FAR

◆ You are working effectively on your chosen language.

◆ You understand the importance of reading.

◆ You understand that this will be a different process from reading in your own language.

◆ You are using your whole life experience to decode the new language and are beginning to read for gist comfortably.

◆ You also know how to read more intensively, when there is the need to understand in greater detail.

◆ You know how to find reading materials and are using them in a way which suits you.

8

Cloning and Adapting

In this chapter we shall look at how:

◆ language is made up of more than just words

◆ one simple sentence you might meet in the first few lessons can lead to many, many more

◆ you can listen and adapt

◆ you can clone a letter or other text written in your chosen language

◆ to ensure accurate structure when cloning or adapting.

MORE THAN JUST WORDS

A language is a good example of where the whole is more than the sum of the parts. It is not just the words themselves which carry meaning, but the way they are put together and they way they relate to each other. We have already seen how even more meaning can be added with facial expression, gesture and other body language. Add tone of voice. And then there is context, the circumstances in which you are using a word. Some languages have words which have different meanings in different situations, and you only know which one is being used usually because it is the only one which makes sense. I once took a group of students in their GCSE year to Germany. We were there to sharpen up their oral practice. We had just been practising going to the doctor's and had learnt such wonders as *diarrhoea* and *constipation.* Imagine their delight as we passed the plumbers' merchants that afternoon, when the writing on the window explained that they stocked everything for constipation. Of course, the German for constipation is the same as the general word for blockage.

When you take another look at your mind-map, you will notice that you are not going to obtain your goals if you do not learn some structures. And as you move away from merely communicating in a type of cave-man language which may sound odd to a native speaker towards something which sounds more like the real thing, you will need to use more complex structures and more of them.

But we're looking in this chapter at making one structure go a long way.

MAKING A LOT OF USE OF A SIMPLE SENTENCE

Let's take something very simple which you may have even learnt in a very early lesson.

The cat sat on the mat.

Look at how you can change one word at a time to make six other simple sentences.

> **A cat sat on the mat.**
> **A *dog* sat on the mat.**
> **A dog *slept* on the mat.**
> **A dog slept *under* the mat.**
> **A dog slept under *a* mat.**
> **A dog slept under a *table*.**

Now imagine that for each word you had six alternatives. These may be presented as a drop-down list on a computer program, or a box diagram in your text book. Or you could make up your own. You might have something like this.

The	cat	sat	on	the	mat
This	dog	slept	in	a	basket
A	pig	ate	off	this	table
That	mouse	ran	under	that	cupboard
Every	rabbit	drank	behind	every	door
No	snake	stood	in front of	his	window

Now how many sentences can you create? If you use every combination? Some of the combinations may be a little odd, but most of them work very well, and the structure will be accurate.

You can go even further with this. Can you think of six descriptive words to put in between the first and the second column and the fifth and the last column? You could have big, small, black, fierce, friendly, hairy animals and old, new, small, large, grey and dark places. Now think of other similar descriptive words – other colours, sizes, characteristics.

Take your calculator and work out how many different sentences you could produce. Just from one simple sentence. You will be amazed.

ADAPTING WHAT YOU HEAR

Often, though, you haven't got time to sit down and work out a table. You want to bring some structure into your speech. You want to speak as accurately as possible. This is where you need to listen for patterns.

It may be a simple matter of not knowing vocabulary. Imagine being in a cake shop. You see something which looks delicious but is not labelled. You point to it and say you would like one of them.

'A *cream horn*?' says the assistant pointing at the same cake.

'Yes, a *cream horn*' you confirm.

In many European and Arabic languages, inanimate objects as well as people have genders, so are masculine, feminine or neuter. This leads to different words being used for it, *the* or *a*. You want to get that right. Let's take another cake example. There is a delightful French choux pastry con-coction which is filled with cream and covered in chocolate. A smaller piece sits on top of a larger one. It is called a *religieuse* because it looks a little like a nun. You not only listen out for the word, but also for the gender, and realise that it is feminine, partly because of the nature of the name and partly because you have recognised the feminine word for 'a'. This might be quite useful if you need to specify *this* or *that religieuse*, as the words for *this* and *that* are also different in French according to gender.

Your structure may be even more complex. But try to listen out for it and reflect it back. You may be asked 'Do you want to go by bus or do you prefer the underground?' You could reply 'I want to go by bus.' Or 'I prefer the underground.' Or you might swap the two structures over if you are feeling really brave and say 'I want to go by underground.' Or 'I prefer the bus.'

Much of speech consists of question and answer. There are two types of questions – ones which need a 'yes' or 'no' answer, and others which need a piece of missing information supplying. In both cases, you use the structure of the question to help you with the structure of the answer. Or, if speaking, you can just give the answer. In an e-mail, you would probably use the reply button, so the original part of the message would still be there. You would give a semi-structured reply. If writing, you need to give the whole structure. Study the following questions and answers.

◆ **Yes/no question.** Did Charles see Mary last Wednesday?

◆ **Speech answer.** Yes, he did.

◆ **E-mail answer.** He did see her last Wednesday.

◆ **Letter answer.** Yes, Charles did see Mary last Wednesday.

◆ **Missing information question.** Where were Charles and Mary?

◆ **Speech answer.** At the hospital.

◆ **E-mail answer.** They were at the hospital.

◆ **Letter answer.** Charles and Mary were at the hospital.

Notice how the basic structure is still there, but that there is a slight change in word order between question and answer. This happens in most languages. Often, when speaking, we indicate that we are asking a question by a change in the way we use our voice. In English, we raise it at the end of the sentence. So we frequently use exactly the same structure in the reply as in the question. Study the two examples below.

> 'He's going where?' 'He's going to the hospital.'
> 'He's going to the hospital?' 'Yes, he's going to the hospital.'

Questions and answers can be very easy! There is a slight snag, though. Often questions contain a 'you' and answers an 'I'. The verb (doing word) which follows will often follow a different pattern. Study the following question and answer.

> 'Are you going to the cinema?'
> 'Yes, I am going to the cinema.'

Not only does the verb change, but it is not a regular pattern. There is good news, however.

1. There are regular verb patterns in every language.
2. The irregular ones tend to be the ones you use most often.
3. When replying in speech, you don't need to give a full answer, and even if you do and you get the structure slightly wrong, the chances are no one will notice as long as they have understood what you mean.

CLONING A LETTER

Accurate structure is far more important in writing. Even when speaking our own language, we make mistakes with structure, often because we are constantly changing the plan about what we are going to say. Most mistakes go unnoticed. When they are more obvious, perhaps because the speaker is using what to them is a foreign language, they are still quickly forgotten if the message is communicated. We once had a young German friend stay with us to improve his English. He actually used a good range of words and phrases, but always kept German word order. He would say such things as 'When go we to the theme park?' and 'I must my clothes wash.' It was rather cute, it didn't prevent us from understanding and those other clues of body language, tone of voice and the context in which he was speaking helped us to understand.

Most written material takes us by surprise and we have to take the message from the words themselves. If the structure is not correct it at best irritates and at worst obscures the meaning. We are also used to reading texts to which the writer has given more thought to the language they are using. In many situations where we write, we want to create a good impression. We do have to get the structure right if we want people to take us seriously.

But there is some good news. When we write, we do have more time and we can use many props: dictionaries, grammar books, our text books and our own notes. And it is very easy to adapt a text you have in front of you to give your version of the same thing.

Study the letter below. The words in *italics* are ones which you could change to make up a text of your own.

Dear *Christine*

How are you? We moved into the new house *yesterday*. It is a *nice detached house* with *three* floors. We have *four* bedrooms, *three* on the *first* floor, and *one* on the *ground* floor. We also have a *study* in the *attic*. *On the ground floor*, we also have *a kitchen, a lounge* and *a dining room*.
   The back garden is big, and has *a lawn, lots of flowers* and *two cherry trees*. The front garden is *quite small* and *pretty*. We don't have a *cellar,* but we do have a *nice, large garage* where we can keep things.
   Hope you are all well. We look forward to hearing from you.

Isabelle

Now look at the following version, and see how I have changed it to describe my own house. Notice that I have put something entirely different at the end. It is good to learn at least two different endings to a letter. It is better if you reply with a different one from the one you have been sent.

Dear *Christine*

How are you? We moved into the new house on *Thursday*. It is a *big linked detached house* with *two* floors. We have *four* bedrooms, *all* on the *ground* floor, *the lounge* on the *first* floor. We also have a *den* in the *garage. On the ground floor*, we also have *a kitchen, two bathrooms* and *a dining area.*

The back garden is *big*, and has *a lawn, lots of flowers* and *a cherry tree and an apple tree*. The front garden is *quite small* and *pretty*. We don't have a *cellar,* but we do have a *space under the terrace* where we can keep things.

Hope everything is all right with all of you. Let us know your news.

Isabelle

Notice how some bits stayed exactly the same – my house happens to have those features in common, and how in some cases I have had to replace a word with a phrase. You may even sometimes have to leave out one part altogether. But you can still construct an effective letter.

One word of caution. You may remember from school days perhaps being encouraged to pretend you had been on holiday even if you hadn't, or pretend to have brothers or sisters even if you didn't. Don't go down that road. You will demotivate yourself. You make better progress in language learning if you are able to talk and write about what is important to you.

Now study the letter below. Decide which words and phrases you might alter to make the letter your own.

Dear Jim,

I started my new job at Kendrick's last week. The offices are in a new building. The journey there is a bit quicker. It takes ten minutes by car. We start work at 8.30 am and finish at 5.15 pm. I miss the flexitime from Broderick's. We have a whole hour for lunch.

The staff can use the staff sports club. We also have a good canteen and a bank on site.

I have got to meet all of my colleagues. I work mainly with Sally Johnston. She has been with the firm for ten years. She is very lively and friendly.

The work is very interesting and I may have the chance to travel abroad soon.

How's your work going? Look forward to hearing from you,

Toni

Now look at Appendix 6 to see which changes I have suggested. Study both letters again. What do you notice about the type of things which I have changed? What *hasn't* changed?

Now try doing one of your own, adapting a text from the language you are studying. You may impress your teacher!

AVOIDING PITFALLS WHEN CLONING

You do have to be quite careful. Be sure that you do not alter the structure. Your texts already give you the pattern of word order, endings on words, how the verb (the doing word) works and how smaller phrases within the sentence are constructed. Just change some of the nouns (naming words) or adjectives (describing words) and only if you are sure of the correct patterns, some of the verbs (doing words).

It is safer to keep to what you know well, but you will be tempted to use the dictionary. That is fine, but you also need to be cautious here. For example, you will often be given more than one word. How do you know which one to use? I remember a student from my A-level German group telling us all that a certain tree had a very fat suitcase. She had looked up the word *trunk*. In bigger dictionaries, clues may be given about the actual significance. A smart trick is also to look the word up again in the other half of the dictionary. Had my classmate done that, she would have found out that *Koffer* was something for transporting personal belongings when you go away from home. Care should also be taken when looking up verbs. The dictionary will only give you the inactive form. You have to make it show who is doing what when, and that means knowing some complex patterns. No dictionary could possibly contain them all.

WHERE TO FIND MATERIALS FOR CLONING

◆ dictionaries – many contain sample letters, both personal and business

◆ your text book

◆ material sent by your learning partner

◆ manuals to do with your work

◆ anything in writing or print.

So, have a go now. Choose a text and make it your own. Whenever you need to write, look for something you can use as a model. Even the Goethe Institute, in its exam for advanced business use of German (level B2/C1 of the European Passport, see Appendix 1) provides a model letter for students to adapt.

THE STORY SO FAR

◆ You are working on your chosen language in a way which suits you, you are well organised and you are developing good language learning habits.

◆ You understand the importance of structure, particularly in writing.

◆ You know how to adapt simple sentences.

◆ You are learning to listen carefully for phrases which you can use.

◆ You know how to use questions to help you structure the answer.

◆ You know how to turn a model piece of writing into your own.

◆ You know how to avoid mistakes and how to use the dictionary effectively in doing this.

◆ You know where to find materials to adapt.

9

Putting in the Backbone

In this chapter you will:

◆ find out how to predict structure

◆ learn why we have grammar

◆ take some of the fear out of dealing with it

◆ get to grips with the basics

◆ find out what you need to know

◆ develop more good habits when writing.

SKELETONS

In the last chapter, we took a look at how to put structure into your language. Hopefully, you are beginning to do that quite well now. It is also possible, however, that you are beginning to get the uncomfortable feeling that the amount of phrases you are going to have to learn is infinite, and that you are never going to manage it or get to know anywhere near enough to sound like a competent speaker.

What if you could get your hands on a system which would enable you to work out what the structure was going to be in any given situation? There is one, and every language has its own. It is called grammar.

Without grammar or structure, language is just a lump of meaningless jelly. Look at this group of words.

Chair caretaker broken window morning find

What are the possible meanings?

Tell the caretaker that we have broken the chair this morning near the window.

We found that the caretaker had broken the window with the chair.

The caretaker found the broken chair near the window.

And many more. What gives the sentences meaning is the way the words relate to each other. And it is structure which causes the relationship. Grammar is the blueprint for the structure, a sort of DNA of the language.

Noam Chomsky recognised that we all need to say the same kinds of things in every language, create the same sort of relationships between words. Part of our brain recognises this, and we fill that up with the conventions of our own language. This can make learning a second language difficult – we often expect the grammar to act in exactly the same way as in our own language and it doesn't. By the time you learn your second foreign language, you are more aware of this. You also know what you need to know.

Grammar is the skeleton of the language. Grammar differs from language to language, just as the skeletons of different species vary. But each animal's skeleton will aid it in breathing, eating, sleeping, moving, reproducing and generally caring for its wellbeing. Each language also needs to enable users to perform the same functions. There will be peculiarities – the French count in a peculiar way because once you showed allegiance to rivalling families in a sort of code and the ones who counted funny became most popular. It is the diversity which makes it all so interesting.

GRAMMAR? HELP!

There is a lot of fear about grammar, and depending a little on your age and what was fashionable in education at the time, this fear has one of three causes.

1. You understand it perfectly – maybe even enjoy analysing it, but you know it doesn't help that much. You did very well at school in your first foreign language – probably French – but feel that you can't speak a word of it. (Remember me and the cheese sandwich?)

2. You don't even know what the word means. You have never been taught any – either in your own language or in a foreign language.

3. You have a vague notion of what it's about, but it seems so complex, and there is so much of it that you'll never be able to get to grips with it, so it's not worth trying.

My answers to this are:

1. Grammar is important in helping to make you accurate in your language, but it is by no means the whole story and should be used alongside the other suggestions I have made.

2. With a limited amount of time, you can only acquire full accuracy by understanding the grammar. It is a short cut to learning structure.

3. There are only actually five things – although with some subdivisions – which you need to know about.

When I first found out about using a learning partner I met a young teacher of German. She was German, though I couldn't believe it. She spoke fluent, accurate English – with a Yorkshire accent! She made the point that she had learnt everything about English grammar by the age of 13 and had spent the remaining ten years just polishing up her knowledge – with a learning partner, of course.

We do need to put grammar in its place – incredibly important, but not all that difficult. That's the bigger picture.

FIVE THINGS YOU NEED TO KNOW
Simple:

◆ verbs

◆ word order

◆ parts of speech (who is doing what to whom where, when and why)

◆ how prepositions work

◆ and how your language shows gender and number.

That's it! Let's look at that a little more closely.

Verbs
When dealing with verbs, we need to consider **mood, voice, person** and **tense**.

The moods
In fact, only a few languages use both moods to any great extent.

◆ **Indicative.** This is what we use most of the time. It is used when we know for a fact that something is true. *The Queen lives at Buckingham Palace.*

◆ **Subjunctive.** This is used when there is some sort of doubt. We rarely use a verb form to express that in English, but *Long live the Queen!* and *If I were a rich man* are two examples. The subjunctive is used a lot in the Romance languages – French, Spanish, Italian – but

Northern European languages tend to express the doubt element with other words.

The voices

Of the two voices, one is rarely used (but I just did) and generally not approved of (there I go again!) except in certain situations (writing books about learning foreign languages, and scientific reports for instance).

◆ **Active.** This is what you use most of the time. *The cat ate the mouse.*

◆ **Passive.** In modern language, this is generally frowned upon. Our example above would become *The cat was eaten by the mouse.* Generally, you use this voice if you do not know who did the action. *Papers were strewn all over the floor.* Some languages even get round this by using the word for 'one'. *One (someone?) had strewn papers all over the floor.* Or they make the verb **reflexive** (the person/thing does the action to itself). So you get *Papers had strewn themselves all over the floor.* Can you see how you are portraying the same idea but using a different structure?

Person

How does your language show who is doing the action? Sometimes it is indicated by the ending on the verb – or at least some alteration of its spelling, or by putting a word in front of it, or sometimes both. You have to know how to indicate that the following people are doing something.

Person	Singular	Plural
1st	I	We
2nd	you	you
3rd	he, she, it, one	they

Many European languages will have two different words for the singular and plural *you,* and there is often another form of you for people with whom you can be fairly familiar – close friends, relations and animals! These two forms of the second person are distinguished as **familiar** or **polite.**

Tense
Tense tells you when something happens, and is divided into **past, present** and **future.**

Present. This, as you could probably guess, is to do with the present. It says what somebody is doing *now.* Most languages just have one verb form for this. But in English we have three versions of it. Can you work out when we use each? And you thought the language you were learning was hard?

> **I read**
> **I am reading**
> **I do read**

All three of those are translated into French by *je lis.*

Past tenses: simple past (sometimes called the preterite). This is used for one-off actions in the past. *He came, he saw, he conquered.*

Imperfect. This is used for continuous and repeated action in the past. In English, it is often characterised by *was . . . ing*. Examples would be:

> **I was watching television when the phone rang.**
> **We used to go to the sea every year.**
> **She came to see me every day.**

Pluperfect. This goes one stage further back into the past. In English, you often get the word 'had' in a sentence.

> **I had already unloaded the shopping and put it all away when the doorbell rang.**

Future tenses: the future. We actually have two forms of this in English, and sometimes use the present tense with a future meaning. This is common in many languages. Compare:

> **I shall go to the cinema this evening.**
> **I am going to go to the cinema this evening.**
> **I am going to the cinema this evening.**

The conditional. In English, this usually contains the word 'would' and indicates something that is by no means certain, that is dependent on some condition. In many languages it is used instead of a future subjunctive. Many languages do not have a future subjunctive.

If I were you, I would go and see him.

Word order

Word order has one of two functions and sometimes both.

◆ It gives meaning to the sentence. This is true in English. In the sentence *the cat chases the mouse* we know who is doing what because of the word order. Some languages put endings on their words to do that.

◆ Most languages have a convention of word order, and it sounds odd if you do not keep to it. On the other hand, changing the word order can be used for effect. In German, you can emphasise something by putting it at the beginning of the sentence, rather than using your voice.

Parts of speech

In all sentences you need to indicate:

The verb. This is the action. Technically, a group of words is not a sentence unless it contains an active verb. Beware, though, some verbs are not very active – like *being* or *sleeping.*

The subject of the verb. The person or thing doing the action.

> **The *cat* sat on the mat.**

You may also have:

The direct object. One of my students described this as the recipient of the action. It is the person or object who receives the action *directly*.

> **I sent *a letter*.**

The indirect object. This is the person or object to which the action is done indirectly. If you are not sure whether an object is direct or indirect, try putting the word *to* into the sentence.

> **I sent *her* a letter. I sent a letter *to her*.**

Adverbial phrases. These tell us where, why, when and how something happened.

Many languages express these ideas by word order (English, French, Spanish for example). Others express them by inflection – adding endings on to words or the markers in front of them, words like *a, the, describing words (German, Latin)*. In both systems there is also a default word order. If the word order is not an indication of the function or importance of words in the sentence, it follows a set pattern.

Prepositions

Or pre (in front of) positions (places). Prepositions usually come in front of words and show the relationship of that word to others in the sentence. For example:

> She was *by* the door.
> He came *to* school *with* his mother.

One main snag with prepositions is that within their own language they often have many different meanings, and they do not translate exactly. For example *by* in English can mean *near to* or *through the means of* (when used with transport). *Mit* in German means *with* or *by* (when used with transport). You have to learn them for each individual language. In inflected languages, different prepositions are followed by different endings.

Gender and Plurals

This is not always as straightforward as in English. We have masculine and feminine for humans and animals only. Of course, ships tend to be feminine. But in French, so are rulers and houses. German has masculine, feminine and neuter, even for objects. You have to know which it is in order to produce sentences with correct structure. There are patterns, and it's worth learning them. Plurals are not always simple either. Several other languages also add the 's' for denoting plural. But there are exceptions, and they are not always the same as our exceptions. And many languages have other methods of indicating the plural. Often, there is more than one pattern, and at some stage you will need to learn them.

And that is all there is to it.

TIME, NUMBER AND QUANTITY

Although in many ways this is more an item of vocabulary than grammar, most languages have a set pattern for these items which are used frequently. It is worth learning them sooner rather than later. They are often listed separately in your course book or your dictionary.

METALANGUAGE – A LANGUAGE FOR TALKING ABOUT LANGAUGE

You will find these terms used in your grammar book, in your dictionary and at the back of your text book. They are often used on computer programs as well. There will be others, but if you understand these, the context in which you meet the others will probably make them clear.

I have listed these expressions alphabetically. You may find it useful to photocopy this page and slip it into whichever book you use the most for help with grammar. I have given an example in each case.

Adjective

This is a describing word. It sometimes comes in front of a noun or sometimes it stands alone.

> The *red* house was very *big*.

Adverb

This is also a describing word, but describes a verb rather than an adjective. In English, it often ends in 'ly' but not always.

> Although he *often* went to the club, this time he walked in *nervously*.

Article

The is the **definite article.**

A or *an* is the **indefinite article.**

Conjunction

These join two sentences together. Sometimes they influence meaning, sometimes they just join.

> He went into town *although* he had no money.
> He went into town *and* met his girlfriend.

Noun

These are naming words. There are **proper nouns,** which usually have a capital letter.

> *John* and *Mary* went to *London*.

Concrete nouns are things which you can touch.

> **He kicked the *ball.***

Abstract nouns refer to items which you cannot see, hear, smell, feel or touch.

> ***Beauty* is in the eye of the beholder.**

Participles
The two main ones are the **past participle** and the **present participle.** They are **parts** of the **verb.**

The **past participle** is part of the **past** tense. In English, it often ends in **t** or **ed.**

> **I have *learnt* my lesson.**
> **They had already *visited* the family.**

The **present participle** is often really an adjective. It gives a description which contains a verb.

> **The *flying* ants were *leaving* their nest.**

It will often also be used as a noun in English, but not in all other languages.

Many people think that *flying* is dangerous now.

We use it also in our continuous present and continuous past tenses but these tenses occur in few other languages.

Pronouns
These take the place of nouns e.g. *she* instead of *the girl*.

CHECKING WRITTEN WORK
You should check each piece of written work very carefully. However, if you have taken in all of the above, you could drive yourself mad trying to check for everything at once and you would probably miss a lot of mistakes anyway. Check for one thing at a time. The list below should help.

1. Verbs – mood, voice, person and tense.

2. Word order – does it show who does what, if that is its function, and does it follow the default pattern?

3. Have you indicated in each sentence who does what to whom?

4. Have you used the correct preposition, and in an inflected language have you used the correct endings?

5. Have you used genders and plurals correctly?

6. Now look for those mistakes you always make! Look through any written work you have had corrected and see if you can find any pattern. There usually is. Look specifically for examples of that in the work you have just completed. In a short while, you will stop making those sorts of mistakes.

KEEP A DIARY

It is good to write a little each day. I often suggest to students that they keep a diary, saying what they have done that day and what their plans are for the next day. I ask them to use the checklist above to revise their work. They then give it in to me to mark. So they tend not to make it too personal.

Obviously, if you are a beginner, this will be more difficult. But could you at least write something, if not a diary, daily? Perhaps using a mixture of 'cloned' material and constructing new language with those grammar points you understand?

USING THE GRAMMAR BOOK

At this point it is a good idea to look through your grammar book and see how your language conveys the grammar points mentioned above. Of course, you will not remember all of it at once. But at least read it through, and you will probably find that you understand it, even if you cannot remember it all.

Then look at any points mentioned that I have not covered. They will still relate to the main points of grammar I have mentioned. Make a note of anything you don't understand and discuss it with your teacher.

If you find grammar easy, you would probably benefit from trying to get it right all the time. You know what you need to know. It is tedious having to look everything up at first. Gradually, however, you become more and more familiar with the structures and they become automatic.

But you may not want to wait. Then it is a matter of learning one grammar point at a time. Mastery of some points brings you closer more quickly to obtaining that all-important level of operational competence (see Appendix 1). I suggest the following order.

SEQUENCE IN WHICH TO LEARN GRAMMAR POINTS

1. The past tense.
2. The future tense.
3. Word order.
4. How parts of speech are shown.
5. Prepositions.
6. The imperfect tense.
7. Using the dictionary effectively (not strictly speaking grammar, but effective use of the dictionary and good knowledge of grammar lead to rapid progress).
8. The pluperfect tense.
9. The passive voice.
10. The conditional tense.

11. The present tense.
12. The subjunctive mood.
13. Genders and plurals (these will have come up in other areas, but this should be work on consolidating them. Almost all languages have patterns which help you work out genders and plurals).
14. How to express wanting, having to, being able to, being obliged to (known as modal verbs).
15. Number, time and quantity (you probably know a lot already, but at this point you should really pin them down).
16. Idioms (language which is grammatically unpredictable). You have probably collected quite a few in your note book. Now deliberately seek them out.
17. Relative pronouns.

And that is it!

Grammar wasn't so bad after all was it?

THE STORY SO FAR

◆ You are making good progress in your chosen language, and really do have many good working habits.

◆ You understand the need for grammar.

◆ You are no longer afraid of it.

◆ You understand the five main points of grammar.

◆ You are learning how to check written work effectively.

- ◆ You are writing a little every day.

- ◆ You have had a good look at your grammar book.

- ◆ You have started to learn the grammar of your chosen language.

10

Eyes Wide Open

In this chapter you will find out:

◆ how to make the most of learning opportunities when in the country of your language

◆ how to learn with your eyes

◆ how to learn with your ears

◆ how to learn with your other senses.

EYES THAT ARE SHUT

Or ears. Whenever I come back from the continent via the Eurotunnel, I become very saddened. Recently I returned from Germany and decided to do a little shopping in Cité Europe, the large shopping centre near the shuttle terminal. I was standing in the queue, waiting to pay at the checkout. There was a young girl in front of me. Her friend joined the queue.

'Excuse me please', she said, as she walked in front of me.

Time for some fun, I thought.

'How did you know I'm English?' I asked.

The girl blushed.

'Well, everybody speaks English', she mumbled.

I took great delight in pointing out that the majority of the people in the shopping centre – despite the vast number of English tourists there – probably did not want to speak English, even if they could. They were French, and didn't they have every right to expect us at least to try to speak their language? We were guests in their country.

Both girls looked a little ashamed. We chatted for a while as we waited to be served. Yes, they were on a school trip and they had done a little French at school. They did know the French for *excuse me please,* and although what they produced was what usually appears in text books rather than what the French normally use, it would have done.

I asked them to listen to some of the French people who were standing in the other queues. It took about 30 seconds for them to establish that most French people said *'pardon'.* if they trod on your toe or needed to get past. We looked at some of the signs around us and tried to work out what they meant. As we got nearer to the till, we listened to what the cashier was saying and how the French customers replied. I am pleased to report that my two new friends managed to be polite in French when they paid for their goods. They were actually using mainly things they had met before but not rehearsed in a real situation. They were adding in a few things they had just learnt.

A little while later I sat in a *salon de thé*. I actually found myself cringing as I heard teachers – perhaps from the same school as the girls – talking in English loudly to make the shop assistant understand. You don't actually need much language to point to a cake you want and order a drink. The language staff from that school could have rehearsed it with their colleagues, and keeping eyes open would have reminded them of the vocabulary they needed as they looked at the menu. If they had kept their ears open, they would have heard plenty of model sentences to help them place their order. I even provided one myself.

THE WRITING ON THE WALL

Are you a compulsive reader? Are you like me – do you read the cereal packet over and over every morning, even though you know exactly what it says? If you see words do you have to read them? If so, and most adults are like this, don't shut down just because you are in a foreign country.

There are words everywhere:

◆ road signs

◆ shop windows

◆ restaurants

◆ adverts

◆ safety instructions on planes, trains and ferries

◆ information signs

◆ washing instructions

◆ manufacturer's instructions.

Some of these signs may be presented in many languages and often visually as well. This is good for helping you to understand. You gain a subconscious knowledge of these words and phrases. A good trick is to make an effort to use and learn a few. Some may end up in your note book. You will find it useful to set yourself a target of how many you want to learn a day.

Some of this material is available in your own country. You may like to set yourself a target of how much to learn a week.

VOCABULARY TEST

One pupil I took on an exchange visit to Germany made very good use of his walk to school with his partner. They tested each other on the words for the objects they saw around them. You could do this at home even. Just look around for ten minutes a day. List down, in English, all the objects for which you do not know the word in your chosen language. Then look them up in your dictionary. Learn them.

When you're in the foreign country, though, this becomes a little easier. You often have more time. If you're on holiday you have more leisure anyway, and this is a very appropriate activity. If you're on business, it can be hectic but there are often substantial chunks of time when you have nothing to do. And you're surrounded by the language, so you may have some of those words in front of you in spoken or written form.

EAVESDROPPING

Become a language detective. Listen to conversations on the bus, in the supermarket queue, and in the bar. Then there are those train and airport announcements. Or the tanoy system in the supermarket, asking for cleaners or supervisors, or telling you of the latest offer. Of course, these are often difficult to understand even in your own language. But when they are clear enough, they are easier to understand than ordinary conversations, because you know roughly what to expect.

If you are a relative beginner, you may find it hard to understand anything you hear. But don't worry. Let the rhythm and intonation of the language wash over you, and when you do speak, using something of which you are sure, try to use the patterns of language you have heard.

Robert was an interesting pupil. He came to France with us on an exchange visit. He had always found French a struggle. Yet he managed to mimic the rise and fall of the French voices around him and the pace of the speech he heard. He spoke gibberish at first, but gradually words began to form. By the end of our time there he was speaking in simple sentences with a perfect accent and pronunciation.

A good source of 'free' listening material is the car radio. As you go along the motorway, signs usually tell you where the local radio channel is found. Often these will be like our own local channels and like our Radio 2 and Radio 5. In other words a good mixture of music and speech. The speech will include short news, weather and traffic reports – just as you'd expect. When the music comes back on, you have time to mull over what you have just heard.

We lived in Holland for two years. Our children attended a school in Amsterdam and we lived in Haarlem. On a good day, the journey took 40 minutes. The radio was on all the time. My daughter was 7 and my son 9 at the time, and they would swear that they didn't understand Dutch. There was a report about three house fires. Two children the same age as mine were rescued from one of the houses. My daughter commented that she thought the children would have been very scared. My son remarked that it was odd that house fires always seemed to come in threes. They were surprised when I pointed out that they had just heard all of that in Dutch. They had a few lessons at school, they listened to the radio for at least an hour and 20 minutes every day – and they listened to Dutch story tapes.

They had some favourite Disney story tapes in English – such as *The Lady and the Tramp* and *The Aristocats*. I managed to find the same ones in Dutch. We listened to the tape and followed the story at the same time. They understood it, because they knew the story and they recognised the pictures. Could you bear to use a story tape?

Then there's television and the cinema. Watch something with which you are familiar that has been dubbed. Like the soaps. It might be quite a joke listening to Harold Bishop speaking fluent French, but you'll understand him. It's likely to be an old episode anyway. You get most of the meaning from the visuals and what you remember, but the language is going in at the same time.

And even watching the soaps produced in the country of your stay is good. Soaps are very predictable and quite visual.

CREATIVE OBSERVATIONS

Your creative writing is usually best when you immerse yourself into a scene and describe what all of your senses perceive. Good writers can create or recall the scene in their mind and then write about what they see, what they hear, what they feel, what they smell and if appropriate, what they taste.

Could you write creatively in your chosen language? Perhaps not easily until you are beyond the level of operational competence (see Appendix 1). But you probably could with the help of cloned structure, your dictionary and your knowledge of your language's grammar. And there are all those other auditory and visual prompts around you. Just stand for five minutes and see what you take in.

If you close your eyes, your other four senses will work harder. We are going beyond the linguistic here. We are taking on the culture too. Yes you will see the road signs and what the shop windows say. But you will also notice how your native speakers greet each other, at which angle they leave their knife and fork on their plates and how their houses have narrower doorways and taller ceilings. Yes, you will hear how they ask for help and express joy and sorrow, how and where they gossip, but you will also hear the different noise their cars make because of the way they drive, that the song birds sing more clearly because there is less traffic and the policemen blow their whistles more frequently. You may notice the warmer air, the rougher road beneath your feet and you may pick up through your shoes the rhythm of the way others walk. You may smell the stronger coffee, the fresher fish or flowers which we do not have. You may even taste and enjoy a drink you have not met before, a new flavour of ice cream and vegetables cooked a different way. You may write about this if you wish. But even if you don't want to or feel you can't, you will begin to take on the habits of the nation along with their language. You will speak more convincingly because of it. You understand these people better, and that also aids your subconscious when it fits the pieces of the puzzle together.

TEN OPPORTUNITIES FOR THE BUSINESS TRAVELLER

1. You are welcomed on to your flight in English and the language of the country to which you are flying. Try to internalise one of the phrases you hear.

2. The safety instructions will also be in both languages. If English is second, try to work out what they say as you hear the foreign language. If you hear English first, pick out a phrase you are going to listen out for.

3. You look through the in-flight magazine. Try to read the section in the foreign language, just referring to the English version if you get stuck.

4. Watch and listen to the cabin crew. There is a general way the cabin crew operates in any culture or language. But they will use some of their own body language.

5. Listen to what they say to passengers and how the passengers respond. Can you clone that? Do this, even if they know you are English and speak English to you. If you're feeling brave, you can make a point of replying in the foreign language.

6. As you wait for your baggage to arrive, do some creative observation. Try to write at least one phrase down in your note book.

7. As you queue to go through customs, if appropriate, and passport control, listen out to the exchanges between the travellers and the officials. Is there something there you can adapt?

8. In the taxi, try out your carefully rehearsed small talk. Listen to the radio. Enjoy the rhythm, the intonation, the pronunciation and the accent, even if you do not understand every single word.

9. As you register at the hotel, take your cues from the people in front of you. Work out what the receptionist is likely to say and how you should respond. Read the walls.

10. In your room, flip through the TV channels. Maybe you find a football match. You know what's going on because of what you see on the screen. You can guess what the commentator is saying because of the way the crowd is reacting. And you find out the words for *goalkeeper, goal, half-time,* if you didn't know them before, because they are scripted at the bottom of the screen. Consciously listen for at least one phrase you will remember. And then let your subconscious do the rest.

And you've only just arrived!

TEN OPPORTUNITIES FOR THE TOURIST

1. You arrive at the first motorway service area in the country which speaks your language. You fill up with petrol. Rehearse your numbers and polite phrases as you go to pay. Take your cues from the people in front of you at the checkout.

2. As you drink your coffee in the restaurant next door, listen to conversations going on around you. Even if you do not understand every word, listen to the music of the language. Try to install its rhythms in your head so that you can use them when you speak. Read the walls.

3. Have a browse through the shop. Is there a manual for your car there? Would it be good to buy one? Or maybe the one which comes with your car has pages in your chosen language. Have a look through before you set off again.

4. Listen to the local radio as you go along. Is there some-one else in the car who is learning the same language as you? Maybe you could try to work out what you have heard as you go along.

5. If you are not the driver, look at signs on the other vehicles and at the side of the road.

6. You see a tourist information point. You stop and go in and have a look. Pick up the brochures which look as if they would be of interest. Later, when you are at your destination, make the effort to read the part written in the language you are studying. Only refer to the English – if there is any – if you can't work it out. And then see *how* it means what it means.

7. You arrive at your destination. You rehearse the phrase you are going to use when you check in. You may be able to take some cues from other people in front of you. If you have to wait, read the walls.

8. You decide to do some shopping. Rehearse your polite phrases. Listen to the supermarket announcements. See if you can mange to buy the offer of the day. Read all the writing you see.

9. You find a piece of advertising put under you wind-screen wipers. Don't bin it. Take it home and read it.

10. You notice a family of native speakers next door. They are a similar 'shape' to your family. Eavesdrop a little on their conversations. Have a few rehearsed polite

phrases, so that you can make a contact. Let your children play together.

And it's only the first evening!

Reread this chapter every time you go abroad until you are doing all of these things instinctively

THE STORY SO FAR

◆ You are making good progress in your chosen language, and you are using a variety of good habits.

◆ You read everything in sight.

◆ You listen carefully and pick up the music of your chosen language along with many new expressions which you hear.

◆ You are using your other senses to help you to become more like the people whose language you are learning.

◆ You are maximising the learning opportunities you meet when abroad.

11

Have a Go

In this chapter we shall:

◆ take the fear out of risking your version of your language on a native speaker

◆ look at language you can try out

◆ create a need to talk

◆ learn to be proactive in looking for language – the magpie instinct in reverse

◆ find sources of help for the above.

TAKING AWAY THE FEAR

We all have some nervousness about trying out the language we have acquired on native speakers. But as with any fear, it is quite useful to look at what is the worst that can happen. It is also good to look at the best which could happen and the stages in between.

The worst

The person to whom we are speaking will not understand a word and actually walk away from us. There are two comments to be made:

◆ you won't actually die because of it

◆ is someone who is so impatient really worth communicating with?

Either way, you don't actually lose.

Boring or frustrating the person to whom you are speaking

Yes, it can be very tiring when you have to speak your own language slowly. You need to enliven that experience up for the person to whom you are speaking. Apologise for speaking so slowly. Have you noticed if you put yourself down a little, others pull you back up? Smile a lot as well. They will be charmed. They will be flattered that you want to use their language.

They may come at you in a full-speed torrent

They may not make any concession to the fact that you are a foreigner and that you have not completely mastered their language. But now it is your turn to be flattered. They were obviously impressed with what you said and how you said it and have assumed you know a lot about their language. You can carry on impressing them if you are prepared.

◆ Anticipate what they might be including in their reply.

◆ Listen out for key words. You could have worked these out in advance.

◆ If the above does not work, ask them to repeat what they have said.

◆ Ask them to speak more slowly.

◆ Tell them you do not understand. They will probably simply repeat what they have said, slow down and use more gesture and facial expression to clarify their meaning.

◆ Explain that you are a learner of their language and are eager to carry on speaking. Thank them for their patience.

The best that could happen

They understand you perfectly and reply with something which is absolutely clear to you. This does pose another problem, however – you now have to be ready to continue the conversation.

Anticipation of what might come next is the key at all times.

TRYING IT OUT

In Chapter 6, we looked at making speaking practice more effective. You remember, you go through it all several times with a partner, changing roles, then changing expression and eventually altering the conversation to some extent. The next stage is to get someone in the know – your teacher or your learning partner – to introduce something un-predictable. You move from the known to the unknown.

However you don't have to be a fortune teller to work out what might come into the unknown. If you're going shopping for greengroceries, you might be invited to try some nice figs that they just got in that morning. You can look out for these sort of exchanges in your own language first.

Then, if you know you are going to face a particular situation soon, you can practise beforehand with a partner from your class, verifying the language you need with your teacher or your learning partner.

Look at the following situation.

You are going on a visit to your twin town and are going to stay with a family similar to your own. You may anticipate that you are going to find yourself in the following situations.

◆ Answering questions about your own family.

◆ Understanding information about the town you are living in.

◆ Being offered food and drink.

◆ Being tired and wanting to go to bed. When you take your language learning seriously and really make an effort to understand and contribute, it can be very tiring mentally. However, you often go to bed and then are unable to sleep. Those new words and expressions are going round and round in your head. But it shows it's working, and then if you dream in your chosen language, you really are on your way.

◆ Having to read a story to a young child in the family.

◆ Talking about your leisure activities.

◆ Checking out times when events are going to take place.

♦ Making an excuse to leave the house because your hostess is looking tired and you want to give them a break.

Let's take just one of those situations and anticipate what might come up. So, you read to a young child in the family. You look at a picture book. The child asks you questions about the story. You also ask the child questions about the story and discuss the pictures. The child then asks you personal questions – for example 'Have you ever seen a wolf?' You ask the child something similar. 'Have you got any pets?'

Of course, other people will come up with different lists and possibly all the rehearsal you have done may not meet the situations you actually encounter. But won't your language have improved? This type of rehearsal differs considerably from the practice mentioned in Chapter 6. There, you move from what is in the text book towards the real-life situation. Here you start with the real-life situation. Both are valid.

This is a very common feature of learning by phone and occurs also in some tailor-made lessons. You negotiate with your teacher what you want to learn. Then you are given patterns to try out, practise and eventually learn by heart.

In other types of courses, you may not be able to determine what you want to learn in advance. However, if you've taken on board all the other techniques mentioned in previous chapters, you will not be starting in a vacuum. You will have a fair amount of language and will have a good idea of how to create extra language. You will only need your teacher or learning partner to verify and help you plug the gaps more quickly.

CHAT UP EVERYONE

If you go to a supermarket in Britain on a Friday night, you will see lines of people not talking to each other. At most they're saying 'Oh, I forgot the cabbage, can you go and get one?', generally just conducting transactions about the essentials. But what a great opportunity that is to talk! Cultivate it in your own language and it will be easier in the new one.

Rehearse a few things you might discuss in such a queue. Even if you just say a little, you may be presented with many good patterns of language which you can later adapt, clone and note in your book. Here's a list for starters.

◆ animals

◆ children

◆ football

◆ the weather (rather British, but the Dutch do it too and it's an easy one to talk about)

◆ the price of petrol

◆ the youth of today

◆ politics (if you're brave).

Dale Carnegie recognised the value of making an effort to get to know people by talking to them about what they found interesting. Connie Ten Boom took tips from his book written in 1936 *How to Win Friends and Influence People.* Talking to a member of the Gestapo about his dog helped her to escape imprisonment. Can you make an effort to open a conversation with everyone you see? Could you admire someone's pet? Talk to a child? (In the presence of their parents of course.) Comment on the lateness of a bus, the beauty of a painting, the delight of a walk in the country with the stranger who is sharing that with you? You'll surely pick up a lot of new language that way. But that might not be the only thing. You will also win new friends and influence people. The language is beginning no longer to be the main point and at the same time becoming even more important. And the habit may spill over into your own language. How much richer your world is going to become!

One of my pupils did better than I expected in his oral exam one year by doing just this. He was bright, and he had a certain linguistic competence. However, he was rather lazy, and I knew he had not done enough work. Sure enough, the evening before the exam, he went out to the park instead of staying at home to revise. How lucky he became, though. He met a group of French girls there. He chatted them up, something he was rather good at, in his somewhat under-developed French. He rehearsed for the oral exam the next day with them. He rehearsed a few other things too. There were several consequences.

◆ He did well in his oral exam.

◆ His French improved generally.

◆ He was invited to France.

◆ He made friends for life – he has actually married one of those girls he chatted up that night.

THE STORY SO FAR

◆ You are continuing to progress in your chosen language, and you really are acquiring a wealth of good learning habits.

◆ You are facing the fear you may have about 'having a go'.

◆ You have started to overcome that fear.

◆ You have learnt how to anticipate and rehearse.

◆ You have started to take every opportunity to hold conversations.

◆ You are beginning to proactively seek productive language.

12

What Next?

In this chapter you will:

◆ look at the extent to which you have achieved your goals

◆ complete an action plan to deal with what is missing

◆ identify anything extra you have achieved

◆ identify what else you would like to know

◆ create a new set of goals

◆ consider whether you wish to continue learning in the same way or whether a change of style might be appropriate.

HOW YOU HAVE BEEN USING THIS BOOK

Perhaps you have read this book from cover to cover, as bed-time reading or to occupy yourself on a train journey. That is great! You are in touch with the bigger picture. Hopefully by now you are bubbling over with excitement and want to try out what has been suggested. You may well want to go back and take a week or so putting into effect what has been described in each chapter. I strongly suggest for the moment, though, that you carry on reading to the end so that you complete the picture.

At some point, though, you will have worked through all of the suggestions and you will be ready to take a look at how much you have achieved of what you set out to do.

LOOKING AT YOUR MIND MAP

Take out that mind map you created when you were deciding which sort of course to follow. Highlight in a bright colour anything which you feel you have not yet managed. Add in another colour anything extra that you are aware you've achieved. You may even be lucky and find that the extras outweigh the deficits. Nevertheless, you will now want to deal with what is missing.

If I look at my original mind map, I will see that I haven't managed to complete everything in the 'put the world right' section. I have, however, also learnt to order food and drink in cafés and restaurants and obtained a fair understanding of recipe books. That makes me feel good. But I still want to do something about putting the world right.

This time I make a list. I have succeeded in reading the newspapers quite well, and I can describe my opinions, but I am still not reacting quickly enough to what other people say and sometimes not even understanding what they say in response to my ideas. I have acquired some of the habits recommended in this book but need to sharpen them a little in this context. Therefore, my list may look like this:

◆ Carry on reading the newspapers and watching current affairs programmes. Try to spend a little more time on this.

◆ Rehearse my argument and the answers to the counter arguments. (I can probably find some good phrases to use in the newspapers and by listening to other people debating.)

◆ Use the dictionary, my teacher, my tandem partner and my knowledge of Dutch grammar to help me structure the language I need to learn.

◆ Make sure I know how to ask people to repeat or speak more slowly.

◆ Always smile, even when disagreeing.

◆ Don't let them speak English to me. I must really insist on speaking Dutch. This is particularly important in the Netherlands.

There is a stage of struggle we all go through. What we need from native speakers at this point is sympathy and patience. We cannot become fluent until we have gone through that stage. The Dutch can be too kind. And whichever language you are studying, you will often meet this sort of helpfulness which is really not all that helpful.

Can you make a similar list? You may never look at the list again after you have made it, but there is something about writing down your goals which affirms them. And it is something to hold yourself to.

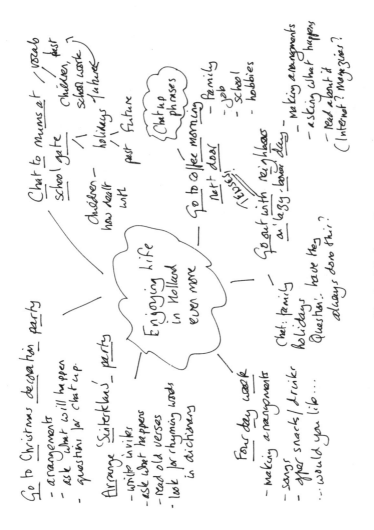

Fig. 4. Mind map 2.

MAKING A SECOND TYPE OF MIND MAP

There are probably certain aspects of life in the countries which speak your language that appeal to you. Maybe you want to go deeper into these. What is the bottom line of why you want to do these things? Make that the centre of your new mind map. Your next layer should list the activities you had in mind. Then come the areas of vocabulary you need, then structures, then parts of grammar, and if there is room, your list of what you must do. Mine looks like the one in Figure 4.

What we have produced is a bit of a side water, a tangent. It is something which is very personal to us. We probably also need to have a more general look at how we are to continue learning our chosen language. If you have worked through this book up to this point, you will have a fair idea of how language learning works. You will probably come up with a similar mind map to the one in Figure 5 for learning Italian – something which I would like to do soon. What may differ the most is the very outer legs, which is very personal and where we recognise our own strengths and weaknesses.

Create your own version of mind map 3 to lead you to a list of tasks you would like to commit yourself to doing.

My list looks like this:

◆ Meet up more often with Sally to practise conversations we have had in class.

◆ Do those conversations with different emotions.

◆ List role-plays to practise with Tania or Sally.

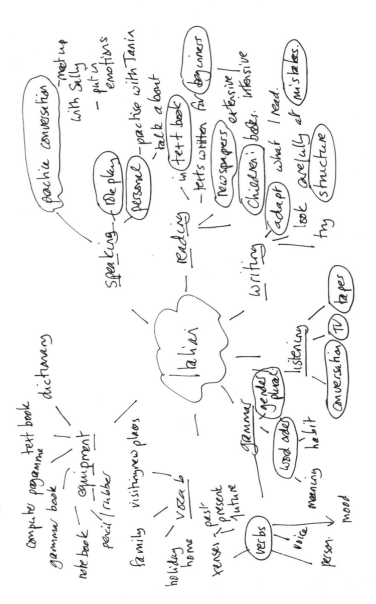

Fig. 5. Mind map 3.

◆ Get some of the readers for beginners.

◆ Look at some children's books.

◆ Read the newspaper for gist, but also pick one or two articles for more intense reading.

◆ Practise writing. Adapt what I have read.

◆ Look carefully at the mistakes I have made.

◆ Practise composing my own structure by writing a little every day.

◆ Use the tapes in the car.

◆ Use the tapes while ironing.

◆ When in Italy listen to conversation around me.

◆ Go through the grammar book – revise the five points of grammar.

◆ Work on holiday homes, visiting new places and talking about the family.

You now have three mind maps and two lists to shape what you might do next. But we haven't finished yet.

METHODS OF LEARNING

Different methods of learning languages have been favoured at different times. The common sense approach has usually overruled, and most teachers have adapted a mixture of them. We all have different preferences, in any case, in the way in which we learn. No method will work, however, unless the learner is engaged in their learning and takes responsibility for it. If you have followed the suggestions in this book, you have sampled a little of all of these methods and you are taking responsibiity for your own learning. Perhaps it is now time for you to look at them more closely and decide which ones help you the most. This is another key feature in you designing the next stage of your study.

Grammar grind

A rather cruel name for something which actually worked quite well. It was favoured up until the mid-sixties and derided in the seventies. You worked systematically through the grammar, starting with the easiest point and coming finally to the most complex. It could leave learners with a thorough understanding of the grammar of the language but unable to use it. Remember my cheese sandwich?

The direct method

This was an attempt to mimic the way we acquire our own language. The teacher would rush into the lesson, shouting 'Good morning, class.' Everyone thought they meant 'I'm sorry I'm late.' Learners under this method were never put off when they went abroad. But neither could they make themselves understood. They did develop some good coping strategies, however.

Drills and patterns

Language stucture is introduced as you need to know it and drilled into you. There is still an emphasis on grammar, but it is not made explicit to the learner. You practise a pattern. New language was often introduced with flash cards, and then you completed the drill on the language laboratory.

It went something like this:

David played tennis.
Hockey
David played hockey.
Swimming
David went swimming.

(You have to learn the exceptions at the same time as the rules!)

As you can see, it is very much like our cloning and adapting activities. But it can be deadly boring and it misses out many other important aspects of language learning. It killed off the language laboratories, as they were used mainly only for this sort of drill. They are coming back now, and are being used to allow learners to listen as well as speak and are often used with videos as well.

Communicative language learning

The message here is communication, communication, communication. Exercises are set up so that the learner is genuinely communicating. The language has worked if the outcome is correct. Often each partner has information the other doesn't. A simple example is that each has half a TV guide. They ask each other such questions as 'What is on Channel 4 at 7 pm?' These are very realistic exercises, but do not always develop grammatical and structural accuracy.

Target language

The teacher speaks all the time in the language you are learning. They do this, however, in a much more conscious way than with the direct method. They always aim to make sure the student understands. At the same time the student becomes used to hearing language as communication. The learner develops coping strategies. Again, little time is available for adding in the knowledge of accurate structure.

Current practice

Teachers talk a lot about good practice. When a system is in development it is often hard to describe. However, most people in language learning would probably agree that you need to:

◆ talk

◆ speak

◆ listen

◆ read

◆ write

◆ understand and use structure

◆ communicate

◆ deal with authentic texts

◆ cope in the real situation.

Courses at the moment are being geared to enable you to be able to do just that and are combining the best elements of all the methods described above. Which areas of the list above need more work?

There are a lot of similarities between learning to play a musical insturment and learning a language. The scales are like the drills. Music theory is like the grammar. You rehearse and practise set pieces until you have them fluent. Then you are able to sight read and you are able to put your own language together, using a grammar reference to help you. You can even compose music and you can write and speak as spontaneously in the new language as in your own. Eventually, you move an audience.

Perhaps that is why one of my most successful students was a friend who used to give me piano lessons in exchange for French lessons. We found many parallels and it was useful to compare how we were learning.

But you may not be musical. There is also an analogy with sport. If you are sporty, you might like to work it out.

You are in a very strong position, if you know what you need to know. You proably do now. Now you need to work out where to find that knowledge and how to acquire the skills which go with it.

LEARNING STYLES AND SETTINGS

Finally, take another look at Chapter 2. You probably don't need to fill in the charts all over again, but look at the advantages and disadvantages of each sort of course and have a look at the different settings in which you could work. Do you feel you want to change something now?

LOOKING AHEAD

You can now plan your next course. You have:

◆ Completed a certain stage of your study.

◆ Looked at your first mind map and identified any gaps (and hopefully congratulated yourself on all the extras you have achieved).

◆ Created a second mind map identifying certain very personal goals.

◆ Created a third mind map with knowledge of how language learning works and identified areas in which you need to work more.

◆ Considered which methods suit you best.

◆ Reconsidered which settings suit you best and the type of course you might now follow.

Now, decide how you want to proceed.

13

Keeping It Ticking Over

In this chapter you will see:

◆ how fluency and accuracy carry on improving

◆ how you can continue to gather language

◆ how you can keep your spoken language fluent

◆ how you can carry on improving your reading

◆ how you can keep on practising writing

◆ how you can carry on improving your listening

◆ how you can adapt life-long habits so that you continue to learn your language without even noticing.

WHERE YOU ARE NOW

You may have completed your course. You might have attained all of your goals. In which case, you are probably delighted. So you may have decided not to carry on with any formal learning. However, you do not want to lose your newly acquired skills and knowledge. What can you do to keep it all ticking over?

WHAT USUALLY HAPPENS

Even if you don't touch your new language for a while, you will not actually forget everything. It may get a little rusty, but it will still be there chugging away like a computer program you had forgotten was running. You will never forget completely.

I used to take a second stage adult French class. Just a few of the members had done one year of French the year before. Most of the rest had completed five years of study at school but many years ago. As soon as they started classes, it all came flooding back, and by the end of the year, they were at least level with where they were when they left school. In some cases they were beyond that.

If you actually do do something to keep your knowledge and skills up to scratch, they will carry on improving.

In my own case, I would say that my French and German are much better than they were when I left university. I may not have the in-depth knowledge any more of the most complex of the grammar, or of the more literary vocabulary. On the other hand, my fluency and ability to deal with everyday language has improved no end. This is probably because:

◆ In 25 years of teaching, I have had almost daily contact with the language.

◆ I have gone on several exchange visits with schools.

◆ I have maintained friendships with speakers of these languages.

◆ I have used several strategies to improve my reading, writing, speaking and listening, and worked in a way that seemed more like pleasure.

In other words, I have continued with the habits I have described in this book.

MORE THAN TICKING OVER

The slightest amount of work you continue to do will move your language skills and knowledge forward. Fluency and accuracy will carry on improving.

You may, for instance, be quite good at negotiating in a shopping situation. Yet the words still stick a little on the way out. Any rehearsal – and the 'real' situation is always a rehearsal for the next time – will make the whole transaction smoother.

You may be communicating well, but are still making tiny grammatical mistakes. The person to whom you are speaking may correct you, either consciously or unconsciously, or they may, without thinking, present you with an accurate pattern of language which you, also consciously or unconsciously, then pick up. What was fluent becomes accurate.

As you continue to look up new words and expressions when you prepare to write, grammatical structures become more familiar to you. You rely less on your grammar book and dictionary. What was accurate but painfully slow becomes fluent.

If you have reached a satisfying plateau, there are nevertheless several things which you can do, which are not onerous, and which will not only maintain your level of knowledge and skill, but will also keep the accuracy and fluency gradually improving.

Carry on gathering

You will probably want to keep your note book or computer file record alive. However, you will not perhaps want to add to it as often as you have been doing. Give yourself a goal now of how many phrases you want to add per month or per week. And always look out for new material when you are abroad.

It is good to spend some time learning as well. Again, you may reduce the frequency. Keep your note book in a place where it is easy to pick up. Leaf through it at odd moments – whilst waiting for the bus, on the train, while you drink a cup of coffee – maybe even when you're stuck in a traffic jam.

Using a computer program

Even if until now you haven't used a CD language course, it may be something you could add on to what you have been doing. Could you agree a time with yourself that you would spend on the language programme every time you begin or finish work on the computer? Five minutes? Ten minutes? Twenty minutes?

Speaking and talking practice

Hopefully you will keep in touch with your learning partner. Agree certain times that you can meet up or speak on the phone. Mix business with pleasure. Complete some focused exercises, where you both agree on what you want to improve, but also just have some relaxing times, when you pick up the language passively.

Maybe you could also arrange to meet up with your former classmates, perhaps once a month. Make it a social occasion. But speak your language all of the time.

And you will no doubt continue to go to the countries which speak your new language. Even though you may feel a little rusty because you haven't used it for some time, you will carry on building on what you already know.

Reading

At this stage you will probably want to do mainly the extensive type of reading. As much as possible read in your new language:

◆ magazines

◆ newspapers

◆ anything written which is of interest in your worlds of work and leisure.

You will find that after a while you forget that you are reading a foreign language. You are reading for information.

It would, however, greatly enhance your reading and general language skills anyway, if from time to time you did a little intensive reading. Take a text and totally unpack it. Make sure you understand every word. Look at the structure in the sentences and why they are built the way they are. Find a few sentences to adapt for your own use. Write a couple of phrases in your note book. Make a decision now about how often you will do this.

Writing with a purpose

You may now feel able to write personal and business letters and e-mails. Even if you have to keep on looking up words and patterns to adapt, you know what you need to know and where to find it. You may be adapting from the dicitonary, ones you have seen or ones your learning partner has sent you. Gradually the communication will become more important than the language you use to effect it. The language just becomes the means to the end. And it won't matter if you make mistakes as long as you communicate correctly.

But you may want to carry on improving your accuracy. In that case, set up some exercises with your learning partner. Ask them to correct certain pieces of writing. You do the same for them. If you both use Word, you can 'track changes', and that will help you become more aware of where you are making mistakes.

You may wish to be even more proactive. Perhaps you could carry on seeking new texts to adapt. Perhaps you could keep a diary. It is better if you can have this sort of work corrected, but even if not, just doing the work is beneficial. You will become more aware of structure and gradually make fewer mistakes.

You may even be tempted to look in the grammar book and really master that backbone of your chosen language. Often, grammar becomes easier after a while. You become more familiar with the metalanguage. Also, once the pressure is off to learn by a certain time, you can take in the information more gradually.

Listening and hearing

Watch TV in your chosen language if you can. This is really more like listening and seeing. Soon you will be enjoying the entertainment rather than being conscious of learning. If you watch programmes produced in the country which speaks your language, you will be taking in some of the culture as well. If you have no access to such channels, can your learning partner send you videos now and then?

Can you listen to other tapes? Libraries often have tapes, which you may borrow, to accompany their language courses. Listening to a different tape from the one which goes with the course you studied can bring you fresh ideas.

And listen, listen, listen when you are in the country where your chosen language is spoken.

Going native

Reread Chapter 10 each time before you go abroad. Let the suggestions made there become a habit. Once they have become a habit, you will no longer be aware that you're working at your language. And your skills and knowledge will continue to grow.

CROSSING THE THRESHOLD

Something happens to all language learners. It happens at different times for different people. Suddenly the struggle stops. If you are fortunate, this may have happened before you stopped your formal lessons. But if you persevere, there comes a point where it stops being a battle, when you stop forgetting old items as quickly as you meet new ones, and all of a sudden the language becomes a tool which is really useful and easily used. There is still some way to go, but now you are comfortable. There is now no going back. And at that point, your language learning really becomes a leisure activity rather than something you are studying.

You may be surprised that this stage did not come early on for me. I actually think it could have come a lot earlier if I had known how the process worked. I saw many of my classmates and later my own students reach that level sooner than I did. But I did reach it, sometime during my A-level study. I had dreamed of being able to use my languages naturally, and suddenly I was able to. I have not looked back since. They are all still improving daily.

IN SUMMARY

◆ You have studied your chosen language, using useful habits, to arrive at a certain level of competence.

◆ You know that your fluency and accuracy will carry on improving, even if you do little more active work.

◆ Your habit of collecting language is so ingrained that you will probably do it for the rest of your life.

- ◆ You know how to practise speaking.

- ◆ You are reading for pleasure and information in your new language.

- ◆ You are communicating in writing and at the same time improving your writing.

- ◆ You are being entertained whilst you improve your listening skills.

- ◆ You know how to make the most of every visit you make to the countries where your chosen language is spoken.

- ◆ You have acquired language learning habits which will allow you to carry on increasing your knowledge and improving your skills.

Well done!

Appendix 1
Levels of Competence

I have created my own definition of a level of competence which is needed for the language you are learning to be useful to you. It resembles the European Languages Portfolio's Level B1, National Curriculum Level 5/6 and would lead to a GCSE grade of C or above. If you are interested in looking at other levels, you may like to study the web sites listed below.

LEVEL OF OPERATIONAL COMPETENCE

General description
You are able to communicate quite well in the language but with some effort. You can operate in everyday situations. You can understand and make yourself understood when working with a sympathetic native speaker.

Talking
You can make everyday transactions – such as shopping, following directions, ordering food in a restaurant and checking into a hotel. You can make polite small talk. These

are not as yet easy, and you still are not all that fluent in these situations. However, you can manage.

Listening
You can understand announcements at trains stations, airports and supermarkets as long as they are reasonably clear. You can understand brief news and weather reports. You can understand a little more on television, because you have visual clues as well. You can follow a quiz programme and a series with which you are familiar, though you will not understand every word.

Reading
You can understand the gist of newspaper and magazine articles, especially when they are in a format with which you are familiar. You can understand personal letters and simple business letters. With extra work, you can understand every word of something written in simple language.

Writing
You can adapt a letter from your dictionary or course book, though you will still have to refer to a dictionary and grammar book. There will probably be some mistakes still, but none that will interfere with communication.

Grammatical awareness
You understand the five points of grammar (see Chapter 9) and how they work in your language. You do not yet know all of the details off by heart, but you are aware of what you need to know.

Body language
You are aware of the body language which goes with your chosen language. You are beginning to use it, even if self-consciously.

Cultural awareness
You are becoming aware of cultural issues which affect the way you use the language.

OTHER LEVEL DESCRIPTIONS
European Language Portfolio, Modern Languages Division, Directorate General IV, Council of Europe, France. http://culture.coe.int/lang

National Curriculum, TSO PO Box 29, St Crispins House, Duke Street, Norwich R3 1GN. http://www.nc.uk.net/servlets/Subjects?Subject=MFL

EXAM BOARDS
AQA, Assessment and Qualifications Alliance Publications Department, Aldon House, 39 Heald Grove, Rusholme, M14 4NA. Tel: (0161) 953 1170. mailbox@aqa.org.uk www.aqa.org.uk

CIE, Cambridge International Examinations, 1 Hills Road, Cambridge CB1 2EU. Tel: (01223) 553554. international@ucles.org.uk www.cie.org.uk

Edexcel, Stewart House, 32 Russell Square, London WC1B 5DN. Tel: (+44 1623 450481). www.edexcel.org.uk

OCR, Oxford, Cambridge and RSA Examinations, Syndicate Buildings, 1 Hills Road, Cambridge CB1 2EU.

Tel: (01223)   552552.   helpdesk@ocr.org.uk www.ocr.org.uk

SEG, Southern Examining Group (part of AQA), Publications Department, Aldon House, 39 Heald Grove, Rusholme, M14 4NA. Tel: (0161) 953 1170. mailbox@aqa.org.uk www.aqa.org.uk

Appendix 2
Language Courses

BUSINESS SCHOOLS

Berlitz, Lincoln House, 296–302 High Holborn, London WC1 7JH. Tel: (+44 207) 611 9640. www.berlitz.com

Ceran, Ceran Lingua Group, Avenue du Château 16, 4900 Spa, Belgium. (+32 87) 791188. www.ceran.com

Goethe Institute, 50 Princes Gate, Exhibition Road, South Kensington, London SW7 2PH. Tel: (+44 207) 596 4000. www.goethe.de/gr/lon/enindex.htm

COMPUTER-BASED LEARNING

Bridge House Languages, 4 Old Bridge House Rd, Bursledon, Hants SO31 8AJ. Tel: (+44 23) 8040 5827. Bridgehouse@btinternet.com
www.bridgehous.btinternet.co.uk

cactuslanguage (French, Spanish, Italian, Portugese in France, Spain, Italy, Latin America and Portugal), Santa Fé Trading Limited, 9 Foundry St, Brighton, East Sussex BN1 4AT. Tel: (+44 1273) 687 697. www.cactuslanguage.com

Learn Foregin Languages On-line, http://members.fortunecity.com/nichokohwk/foreignlanguages.html

Linguaphone, Linguaphone Institute Ltd, Liongate Enterprise Park, 80 Morden Road, Mitcham CR4 4PH. Tel: (+44 (0)20) 8687 6210. LangSupport@linguaphone.co.uk www.linguaphone.co.uk

Lingulearn. Tel: (+44 1273) 597169. info@lingualearn www.lingualearn.co.uk

Net Learn Languages, 1 Roman House, 9/10 College Terrace, London. Tel: (+44 20) 8981 1333. enquiries@nll.co.uk www.nll.co.uk

Prima Language Service Ltd Victoria House, Victoria Road,
. Farnborough, Hants GU15 7PG. Tel: (+44 1252) 377595 info@proma-global.com www.prima-global.com

HOME STAY

Ramapo (Spanish), The Study Abroad Office, Ramapo College of New Jersey, 505 Ramapo Valley Road, Mahwah, NJ. Tel: (07430 + 1(201)) 684-7262. E-mail: studabrd@ramapo.edu www.ramapo.edu

Tlataoni (Spanish), Calle Primera Norte No 8, Buenavista de Cuéllar, Gro., México, C.P. 40330. info@eltlatoani.com www.eltlatani.com

RESIDENTIAL COURSES

cactuslanguage, as above

Don Quijote (Spanish in Spain and Peru), PO Box 218, Epsom, Surrey KT19 0YF. Tel: (+44 20) 8786 8081. dquk@donquijote.org www.donquijote.org

Enforex (Spanish), c/o Lanacos (see below).

International Language Schools (Chinese, French, German, Italian, Spanish and Russian in China, France, Germany,

Spain, Italy, Latin America and Russia), 1–3 Farman Street, Hove, East Sussex BN3 1AL. Tel: (+44 1273) 201 410. languages.gb@ef.com www.ef.com

Lanacos (French, German, Italian and Spanish in France, Germany, Italy and Spain), 64 London Road, Dunton Green, Sevenoaks, Kent TN13 2UG. Tel: (+44 1732) 462 309. languages@lanacos.com www.lanocos.com

Language Courses Abroad (French, German, Italian and Spanish in France, Germany, Italy, Latin America and Spain), 67 Ashby Road, Loughborough, Leicestershire LE11 3AA. Tel: (+44 1509) 211612. Languagecourses.abroad@btinternet.com www.languagesabroad.co.uk

Vis à vis (French in France, Belgium and Canada), 2–4 Stonleigh Park Road, Epsom KT19 0QT. Tel: (+44 20) 8786 8021. dquk@donquijote.org www.visavis.org

SCHOOLS OFFERING TAILOR-MADE COURSES

Bridge House Languages, 4 Old Bridge House Rd, Bursledon, Hants SO31 8AJ. Tel: (+44 23) 8040 5827. Bridgehouse@btinternet.com www.bridgehous.btinternet.co.uk

Prima Language Service Ltd, Victoria House, Victoria Road, Farnborough, Hants GU15 7PG. Tel: (+44 1252) 377595. info@proma-global.com www.prima-global.com

LOCAL AUTHORITY COURSES

Consult your local council, and look out for adverts in the local press. Libraries often also have details.

THE OPEN UNIVERSITY

Walton Hall, Milton Keynes MK7 6AA. Tel: (+44 1908) 274066. www.open.ac.uk

UNIVERSITY CONTINUING EDUCATION DEPARTMENTS

Aberystwyth University, The Centre for Continuing Education, 10/11 Laura Place, Aberystwyth, SY23 2AU. Tel: (+441970) 621580. http://www.aber.ac.uk/courses/ conted.shtml conted@aber.ac.uk

University of Bath (in Swindon), Tel: (+44 1793) 690909. http://www.bath.ac.uk/swindon/parttimecourses/ languages.html

Bristol University, Tel: (+44 117) 928 7172. http://www.bris.ac.uk/cms/ppo/modern_languages.htm b.hanrahan@bris.ac.uk

Cambridge University, 11 West Road, Cambridge, CB3 9DP. http://www.langcen.cam.ac.uk/index.htm

City University, Northampton Square, London EC1V 0HB. Tel: (+44 20) 7040 506. http://www.city.ac.uk/conted/ cfa/htm

Coventry University, School of International Studies and Law, Coventry University, Coventry CV1 5FB. Tel: (+44 24) 7688 8256. http://www.coventry.ac.uk/acad/isl/ulp/htm isladmin@coventry.ac.uk

Liverpool University, The University of Liverpool, 19 Abercromby Square, Liverpool L69 7ZG. Tel: (+44 151) 794 6900. http://www.liv.ac.uk/conted/ conted@liverpool.ac.uk

Manchester University, Tel: 0161 275 3273. www.man.ac.uk/ cce/courses/modlang.htm Julia.Fenton@man.ac.uk

Portsmouth University, University of Portsmouth

Information Centre, Guildhall Walk, Portsmouth, Hampshire PO1 2RY. Tel: (+44 23) 9284 3960. http:/www.port.ac.uk/courses/fe/search/index.htm james.mellor@port.ac.uk
Sheffield University, 196–198 West Street, Sheffield S1 4ET. www.shef.ac.uk/till
Southampton University, Tel: (0800) 085 63 61. http://www.newcollege.soton.ac.uk/Part-time/ basic_parttime_lang.htm.htm
Sussex University, University of Sussex, Falmer, Brighton BN1 9RH UK. Tel: (+44 1273) 606755. www.sussex.ac.uk/central/parttime.shtml information@sussex.ac.

More and more universities are adding languages for mature students. Therefore it is also worth checking your telephone directory which should list all departments of your nearest university. If you cannot find a continuing education department, try the main switchboard. Or type in 'X+University+ continuing+education' or 'lifelong learning' into the search box on your favourite internet search engine.

Also try http://www.education-world.com/higher_ed/ college.shtml.

Appendix 3
Materials

GENERAL

Authentik (GCSE – Advanced Level in French, German, Italian and English), 27 Westland Square, Dublin 2, Ireland. Tel: (+353 1) 677 1512. info@authentik.ie www.authentik.com

BBC Education PO Box 1922, Glasgow G2 3WT. Tel: (08700) 100 222. www.bbc.co.uk/schools

Chancerel International Publishers Ltd (materials for the business learner), 120 Long Acre, London WC2E 9ST. Tel: (+44 20) 7240 2811. Chancerel@Chancerel.com www.pourparleraffaires.com

Collins, 77–85 Fulham Place Road, London W6 8JB. Tel: (+44 8700) 900 20 50. queries@harpercollins.com www.fireandwater.com

LCP, FREEPOST CV2662, Lemington Spa CV31 3BR. Tel: (+44 1926) 886914. orders@lcpuk.co.uk www.lcpuk.co.uk

Nelson Thornes, Delta Place, 27 Bath Road, Chetlenham, Gloucestershire GL33 7TH. Tel: (+44 1242) 221914. cservices@nelsonthornes.com www.nelsonthornes.com

COMPUTER COURSES
urolog www.aurolog.com
Encore www.encoresoftware.com
Eurotalk www.eurotalk.co.uk
GCSE www.gsp.cc
MindMan Personal www.mindman.com
Personal Tutor www.bridgehouse.btinternet.co.uk
Transparent www.transparent.com
Urban Spanish (Spanish) www.towerofbabel.co.uk
wordProf (French vocabulary for all levels) www.wordProf.com

DICTIONARIES
Collins, as above.
Oxford, Oxford University Press, Great Clarendon Street, Oxford OX2 6DP. Tel: (+44 1865) 267652. kaila@oup.co.uk www.oup.com

GRAMMAR BOOKS
Collins, as above.

LISTENING MATERIALS
Authentik, as above.
Champs-Elysées (reading and listening materials for adults, beyond operational competency in French, German, Italian and Spanish), FREEPOST LON 295, Bristol BS1 6FA. Tel: (0800) 833 257. www.champs-elysess.com

READING MATERIALS

Authentik, as above.

Champs-Elysées, as above.

International Press Network (supplies newspapers and magazines in Arabic, French, Gallic, German, Italian and Spanish), 1–3 Dufferin Street, London EC1Y 8NA. info@pressnetwork.com www.interpressnetwork.com

Appendix 5
Useful Web Sites

http://www.alphabetsoupfli.com/
http://www.bonjour.org.uk/default.htm
http://www.centralbureau.org.uk/
http://www.christusrex.org/www1/pater/
http://www.eurocosm.com/
http://www.foreignlanguagehome.com/
http://www.hallo.org.uk/
http://www.hola.org.uk/
http://www.ika.com/cuentos/menu.html
http://www.languages-on-the-web.com/
http://www.penpalnet.com/
http://www.slf.ruhr-uni-bochum.de/
http://www.steadylearning.com/
http://www.vokabel.com/
http://www.worldpath.net/~hiker/iloveyou.htm l

Appendix 6
Cloned Letter 2

Dear *Jim,*

I started my new job at *Kendrick's last week.* The *offices* are *in a new building.* The journey there is *a bit quicker.* It takes *ten minutes by car.* We start work at *8.30 am* and finish *at 5.15 pm.* I miss the *flexitime* from *Broderick's.* We have *a whole hour* for lunch.

The staff can use *the staff sports club.* We also have a *good canteen* and *a bank on site.*

I have got to meet all of my colleagues. I work mainly with *Sally Johnston. She* has been with the firm for *ten years.* She is *very lively* and *friendly.*

The work is *very interesting* and I may have the chance *to travel abroad* soon.

Hope everything is alright with you all. Let us know your news.

Toni.

Index